ESSENTIAL HISTORIES

Caesar's Gallic Wars
58–50 BC

Kate Gilliver

OSPREY PUBLISHING
Bloomsbury Publishing Plc
Kemp House, Chawley Park, Cumnor Hill, Oxford OX2 9PH, UK
29 Earlsfort Terrace, Dublin 2, Ireland
1385 Broadway, 5th Floor, New York, NY 10018, USA
E-mail: info@ospreypublishing.com
www.ospreypublishing.com

OSPREY is a trademark of Osprey Publishing Ltd

First published in Great Britain in 2024

The text in this edition is revised and updated from: ESS 43: *Caesar's Gallic Wars*
(Osprey Publishing, 2002).

Essential Histories Series Editor: Professor Robert O'Neill

ISBN: PB 9781472862013; eBook 9781472862020; ePDF 9781472862006;
XML 9781472861986; Audio 9781472861993

24 25 26 27 28 10 9 8 7 6 5 4 3 2 1

Cover design by Stewart Larking
Maps by The Map Studio, revised by www.bounford.com
Index by Mark Swift
Typeset by PDQ Digital Media Solutions, Bungay, UK
Printed and bound in India by Replika Press Private Ltd.

To find out more about our authors and books visit www.ospreypublishing.com.
Here you will find extracts, author interviews, details of forthcoming events and
the option to sign up for our newsletter.

CONTENTS

INTRODUCTION

Between 58 and 50 BC Roman armies commanded by Julius Caesar campaigned against and defeated the Celtic tribes of northern Europe and extended Roman influence into Britain and Germany. Through a series of battles, sieges and the brutal crushing of revolts, the Romans conquered a vast area of western Europe equating to modern day France, Belgium, Luxembourg and Germany to the west of the Rhine, an area of over 300,000 square miles. The war brought huge numbers of casualties and mass enslavement of the Gauls, and led to profound changes in the societies of the Celtic tribes with the gradual establishment of Roman provincial government and development of Gallo-Roman cultures over the following centuries. For Rome, the conquests brought security to its northern frontiers and provided a launchpad for future incursions to Germany and Britain, but also gave Julius Caesar wealth, power and a loyal veteran army that allowed him to march on Rome, wage civil war and make himself dictator, paving the way for the rule of emperors in Rome.

The conquest of Gaul took place amid political and cultural change in both Gaul and Rome. By the mid-1st century BC parts of Gaul were already starting to become urbanised and 'Romanised' through influence from the Roman province (Provence) in the south and through Roman traders who were becoming very active in Gaul, particularly in the southern and central areas. Wine, pottery and other luxury goods associated with Roman lifestyle were imported, and grain, iron, hides and slaves exported. Politically, Gaul was fragmented; inter-tribal warfare was common and this gave the advantage to Rome through the initial phases of conquest: many Gallic tribes often struggled to form sufficiently powerful alliances to counter Roman

Aureus (gold coin) with head of Julius Caesar, minted by Octavian in northern Italy, 43 BC. (Photo by Hoberman Collection/Universal Images Group via Getty Images)

advances whilst others such as the Aedui and Remi joined with the Romans, providing troops, supplies and valuable intelligence.

Rome too was experiencing political turmoil with the oligarchic system of government facing pressures from within. Rome had expanded its territories throughout the Mediterranean world but its political system was designed for a small city-state and it struggled with the demands of ruling an empire. That required powerful and independent provincial governors and legions retained under arms for extended periods. Leading politicians vied with each other for power and gathered support from their peers, the common people, and the armies that they commanded in the provinces. It was inevitable then that Julius Caesar, appointed to the governorship of Cisalpine Gaul (northern Italy) and Dalmatia in 59 BC would seek to campaign somewhere. When the governorship of Transalpine Gaul (southern France) was added to his command and the Helvetii in Switzerland began a huge migration, Caesar decided to campaign in Gaul.

The Gauls had no tradition of recording their own history in literary form, so we rely on Roman sources to understand the conquests. Caesar's own narrative, his *de Bello Gallico*, is easily accessible and is the most detailed eye-witness account of campaigning from the Roman world, a unique insight into warfare from the commander's perspective. Caesar probably published these commentaries annually, ensuring that Rome remained captivated by his exploits despite his physical absence from the city. Caesar was his own, extremely able spin-doctor and ensured his audience got a one-sided and very favourable version of events. He stressed the magnitude of Roman victories and his own part in them, and downplayed the reverses and the tense situations when he pushed his luck. The biographers Suetonius and Plutarch and historians Appian and Cassius Dio cover Caesar's campaigns in Gaul with varying degrees of detail; they provide a balance to the highly favourable account of Caesar himself, as they were not just reliant on Caesar's narrative. Cassius Dio in particular notes the aggression of the opening campaigns and a reliance on engagements rather than diplomacy.

Archaeological evidence illustrates some of the events described in the narratives. Sites like Alise-Sainte-Reine in the Côte-d'Or, identified as Alesia, suggest that the scale of operations described by Caesar may be exaggerated. New finds help to advance our understanding of the campaigns and their nature: work on Gallic *oppida* (fortified town that were usually administrative centres) such as Châteaumeillant has revealed the sophistication of rampart construction to counter Roman military engineering. Roman camps and fortresses have not been discovered in sufficient numbers to assist significantly in the reconstruction of narratives of the campaigns, but new finds help to expand our knowledge: a legionary camp at Hermeskeil probably belongs to the campaigns of Labienus against the Treveri in the late 50s BC, and archaeological evidence for atrocities reported in the literary sources have come to light in the Netherlands.

Within three years of invading, Caesar was able to declare the whole province conquered and he led his army into Germany and across the channel to Britain, expeditions that provoked shocked admiration back in Rome. Gaul may have been conquered but the Gauls were not. The last years of Caesar's command were spent dealing with resistance and revolt culminating in the major uprising led by Vercingetorix, who was finally able to unite the tribes. The Gauls pursued a guerrilla campaign and a scorched-earth policy while the Romans countered with sophisticated siege engineering, capturing key Gallic strongholds, with the climax to the revolt coming at Alesia and the surrender of Vercingetorix after the failure of a massive Gallic relieving army to lift Caesar's siege.

Reconstruction of the Roman siege works at Alesia, based on archaeological evidence and Caesar's description; Muséoparc d'Alésia. (Prosopee, Wikimedia Commons, CC BY-SA 3.0)

Although it was not until the reign of the first emperor, Augustus, that Gaul was fully pacified (and even then there are indications of resistance into the mid-1st century AD), the Gauls were never able to unite effectively again. Gaul became several Roman provinces, evolving after five centuries into the Frankish kingdoms and eventually becoming France. Julius Caesar went on to wage a civil war and make himself dictator of Rome, only to be assassinated in 44 BC.

BACKGROUND TO WAR
Building an empire

Romans and Gauls had been clashing for centuries before the conquest of Gaul in the 1st century BC, but for long periods they had also experienced comparative peace as neighbours or near neighbours. Celtic or Gallic tribes (as the Greek writers called them) migrated into northern Italy during the late 5th and early 4th centuries BC with some tribes settling, particularly around the fertile Po valley. The first major encounter between Rome and these Celtic tribes of what is known as the La Tène culture came in the early 4th century BC. They penetrated south into Etruria and Latium (Toscana and Lazio) where the invaders captured and sacked some of the largest cities including the important Etruscan centre of Veii only a few miles north of Rome. In 390 BC Rome's field forces were defeated and the poorly defended Rome captured by the Gauls. Only the citadel held out: according to tradition, when the Gauls tried to scale it in a surprise night attack, the guard dogs failed to bark and it was only the honking of geese (kept on the Capitol because they were sacred to Jupiter) that awoke the guards who then repelled the attack. The story may not be true, but after sacking Rome, or being paid off by the Romans, the Gauls withdrew. They were defeated shortly afterwards by Camillus, the great Roman general who is traditionally

This 4th-century BC funerary stele from Etruria shows a naked Gallic warrior in combat with an Etruscan cavalryman. (Photo By DEA / A. DAGLI ORTI/De Agostini via Getty Images)

credited with making fundamental changes to the Roman army in order to deal with this new Gallic threat. The sacking of Rome was never forgotten, and Romans remained haunted by a kind of collective fear of hordes of barbarians returning to destroy the city. The sack, along with the long subsequent history of violent encounters between the two cultures, formed part of the background to Caesar's conquest of Gaul.

During the 150 years after the sack, Rome was gradually able to establish superiority over much of the Italian peninsula, ejecting several of the Gallic tribes from lands to the north of Rome. Between the First and Second Punic Wars (during the 3rd century BC) this conquest of Italy extended to the north as a coalition of Gallic tribes from northern Italy and across the Alps moved south, only to suffer a devastating defeat at Telamon in 225 BC which broke Gallic resistance in Italy. In the following five years much of the territory beyond the river Po was incorporated as the province of Cisalpine Gaul (Gaul on 'this' – the Roman – side of the Alps), and Roman colonies were founded at Piacenza and Cremona. The final reduction of this new province had to wait until after the Second Punic War and the repulse of the Carthaginian forces under Hannibal. After the first big Roman defeat at the hands of Hannibal at the Trebia in 218 BC, Gallic mercenaries flocked to join Hannibal and served with him through much of the Italian campaign. But after defeating Carthage, Rome turned back to north Italy and punished the tribes who had fought against them. The whole of Italy as far north as the Alps was incorporated as Roman territory and further colonies were created at Bologna and Parma. By the mid-2nd century BC Rome was ready to move into France, having secured its occupation of the whole of Cisalpine Gaul.

The excuse came in 154 BC when the Greek city of Marseilles requested help from Rome against raids from Liguria. The Roman response included the establishment of a small veteran settlement at Aix en Provence, which irritated the powerful Allobroges tribe nearby on whose territory it was founded. They and their allies, including the Arverni, were defeated in a series of campaigns fought by Domitius Ahenobarbus and Fabius Maximus. Fabius inflicted a crushing defeat on the Gauls in 121 BC, claiming the quite extraordinary (and highly unlikely) casualty figures of 120,000 Gallic dead to only 15 Roman. The new province of Transalpine Gaul was created, which the Romans frequently referred to as simply 'The Province', from which modern Provence gets its name. As in Cisalpine Gaul, colonies were founded, at Nîmes and Toulouse, and a road was built, the Via Domitia, linking Italy with Spain. As well as leading to the creation of another province, the campaign to assist Marseilles brought Rome into alliance with the Aedui, a Gallic tribe of modern Burgundy who were

Section of Roman road near Geneva. Roman legionaries were engineers and road-builders as well as fighters, creating the infrastructure for conquest and provincialisation. (Stuart Wheeler, Flickr, CC BY 2.0)

also allied to Marseilles. The existence of the new province and a formal alliance with the Aedui provided Rome with opportunities for further intervention in Gaul and the affairs of the Gallic tribes, but any further expansion was brought to a sudden stop by the arrival in southern Gaul of the Cimbri and Teutones. These migrating Germanic tribes offered serious resistance to Rome, defeating successive consular armies in the late 2nd century BC. They were eventually beaten by the hugely successful Roman general and consul Marius, but as with the Gallic sack of 390 BC, the experience left scars on the Roman psyche. Future Roman attacks and campaigns against Germanic tribes were presented as retribution for the defeats and casualties of the 2nd-century incursions.

By the 1st century BC many of the tribes in Gaul were becoming urbanised, particularly those in the south where they came under the cultural influence of Marseilles and then, with the establishment of the province of Transalpine Gaul, Rome. Although Caesar uses the word *oppidum* to describe hill forts, he also uses it for defended settlements that were not on hills. Some of these could have been described as towns even by Romans who might have regarded Gaul and nearly everything about it and its inhabitants as 'barbaric'. Avaricum (Bourges) for example had an open space which Caesar called a forum and may have had civic buildings; it had a huge defensive wall and its inhabitants regarded it as the most beautiful city in Gaul. Cenabum (Orleans) had a series of narrow streets which may well

Despite the Roman perception of Gauls as 'barbarians', many Gallic tribes had well-established towns (*oppida*) such as Bibracte near Dijon, the capital of the Aedui. (PHILIPPE DESMAZES/AFP via Getty Images)

have been planned: Gallic towns were starting to adopt the grid plans of Mediterranean cities. Evidence of coin manufacture at important *oppida* suggests that they may have been tribal capitals, indicating a degree of political centralisation; Bibracte, for example, seems to have been the 'capital' of the Aedui, who were a fairly centralised tribe although plagued by factions. Other tribes who lacked this degree of centralisation might have been

considered culturally backward by the Romans, but this added to their military reputation: Caesar considered the Belgae to be the bravest warriors of the Gauls because they were furthest removed from Roman influence. Their lack of centralisation also meant that they could be harder to conquer, as Caesar was to find when fighting tribes like the Veneti and Menapii who appear to have lacked a single centre of occupation and wealth.

Water transport was essential for both the conquest of Gaul and trade in the provinces Rome established there. (Historia / Alamy Stock Photo)

One of the main reasons for the Greek and Roman influence on the Gallic tribes was trade. Marseilles was a significant centre of trade, and though Gallic tribes and Rome regularly fought each other, that did not prevent a huge amount of trade taking place between them well before the conquest under Caesar. Romans imported raw materials from Gaul, including iron, grain, hides and slaves, the main source of the latter being regular inter-tribal warfare that took place between both Gallic and Germanic tribes. In exchange, the Gauls (or at least the Gallic elite) received luxury goods and foods, and significant amounts of wine. Wine had become a key symbol of wealth, status and 'civilisation', though the historian Diodorus Siculus says that the Gauls drank it neat, rather than diluted with water in the Roman style. Hence, although they were adopting the 'civilised' customs of the Mediterranean, Diodorus makes it clear that they were still 'barbarians' because they did not know how to drink it properly. He goes on to say that wine had become such a valuable commodity that the exchange rate for an amphora of wine was one slave, although there were certainly plenty of slaves around. There must have been many Roman merchants already in Gaul before Caesar's campaigns, including a community of citizens at Cenabum. Some of them were of high status and belonged to the Roman Equestrian order, the influential class immediately below senatorial rank, itself a prime source of new senators. They might expect to benefit from the opportunities conquest would bring, especially if they provided assistance in the form of intelligence and supplies for the Roman army.

Many of the tribes who had come under greater influence from the Greek and Roman cultures to the south were ruled by oligarchies with annually appointed magistrates. The spreading centralisation and tendency towards urbanisation made such tribes easier targets for Rome, and internal factions within them helped the Romans too. In the mid-1st century BC the Aedui were divided between a pro-Roman faction under

Diviciacus, and those who opposed the Romans led by his brother Dumnorix. Dumnorix held a monopoly over the wine trade on the Saône, a tributary of the Rhône, and probably resisted the growing Roman influence for economic as well as political reasons. His influence came from his wealth and his position as a druid: druids held high social status in Celtic society which could bring them political influence. According to Caesar, Dumnorix was attempting to increase his power-base within the Aedui not just because he was opposed to the tribe's pro-Roman stance, but because he was keen to seize power and make himself king. It was valuable to Rome that the Aedui remained united and powerful allies of Rome among the Celtic tribes of Gaul, and the squabbling between the two brothers must have given Rome cause for concern.

Silver coin of Dumnorix of the Aedui. He holds the head of a defeated enemy in his left hand. (akg-images / Pietro Baguzzi)

But the Aedui were coming under pressure from other tribes in Gaul in the 1st century BC. They were a powerful tribe with other lesser tribes under their protection and they had a long-standing rivalry with their neighbours, the Arverni. This rivalry came to a head in 71 BC when the Arverni attacked, along with their allies the Sequani, and German mercenaries from the Suebi whom the Sequani had invited along. Once the Aedui were defeated the German mercenaries under their king Ariovistus turned on their erstwhile allies and seized much of the Sequanian territory. These events had several consequences. Rome failed to assist its allies, the Aedui, which must have damaged its reputation among the Gallic tribes, and Germans were now settling in Gaul near the territory of the Helvetii. This must have seriously worried the Helvetii who had already been forced into Switzerland by earlier migrations of Germanic tribes and they prepared to evacuate their homelands and migrate themselves, to western France.

In 61 BC the Roman senate had confirmed its support for the Aedui, but still failed to act. The Roman people were probably expecting some kind of involvement with Gaul in 60 BC though, perhaps military support for the Aedui. Probably because of concern about the huge migration which was obviously about to take place, preparations were made in Rome, including the holding of a military levy. During his consulship in 59 BC Julius Caesar had bought off the Suebic king Ariovistus with diplomatic gifts and the title of Friend of the Roman People. It was not an unusual move for a leading politician to make alliances with kings outside the Roman empire, especially kings of neighbouring territories who might supply additional troops for a campaign. During his year as Consul, Caesar also engineered for himself the appointment as governor of Cisalpine Gaul and Illyricum (the Adriatic coast of Dalmatia); when at the end of the year the governor of Transalpine Gaul suddenly died, Caesar was given that command as well. The forces under his command consisted of one legion based in Transalpine Gaul and three more legions that were in garrison at Aquileia in north-east Italy, based there because of the potential threats from Ariovistus and the Helvetii to the north and Dacian tribes to the north-east. Caesar may have been planning a campaign against Illyricum initially, but the late addition of Transalpine Gaul to his command opened up a better option for large-scale conquest against a traditional enemy of Rome.

Caesar was an ambitious politician and in order to dominate politics as a senator in Rome in the 1st century BC, it helped to be extremely wealthy (to bribe the electorate), and to have a great military reputation. Of his two allies and rivals, Marcus Crassus was fabulously rich, and Pompey was both wealthy and Rome's leading general after conquering much of Spain and Turkey. On his appointment as governor of Cisalpine and Transalpine Gaul, Caesar was pretty much broke and had had little opportunity to establish himself as an able general. Conquest of a new province would allow him both to enrich himself and to impress the public in Rome with his military ability. There was no doubt at all that Caesar would campaign somewhere and conquer a new province, either on the eastern Adriatic coast or in Gaul. It happened that there were two convenient pretexts for launching operations in Gaul: the Helvetii began their migration just as Caesar was taking over command, and there was still the matter of Rome's previous failure to support its allies the Aedui. If they requested assistance, particularly against the German king Ariovistus, Caesar could justifiably intervene. At the start of 58 BC the new governor of Cisalpine and Transalpine Gaul was still in Rome when news arrived of the movement of the Helvetian tribes.

WARRING SIDES
Discipline vs. spectacle

The Roman army that campaigned in Gaul in the 1st century BC was to all intents and purposes a professional one, with many soldiers in the legions regarding their military service as a career. The soldiers were equipped, trained and paid by the state, often serving for many years at a stretch. The Gallic armies were very different. Gallic warfare was based on the values of a warrior society; while the elite warriors may have been able to spend time raiding neighbouring tribes and may have possessed high quality arms and armour, tribes were unable to maintain armies for long because of the lack of a sophisticated supply system and the need for many of those fighting to return to their fields. The Roman conquest of Gaul was a clash between two cultures employing very different methods of waging war.

The Romans

The Roman army was made up of two types of troops: the legions composed of Roman citizens, and auxiliary units of non-Romans who fought alongside Roman generals because of treaty obligations or out of choice. When Caesar started his governorship he had four legions assigned to his command, but he immediately began recruiting in northern Italy, and possibly not being too strict about the citizen status of his recruits since much of the population of Cisalpine Gaul did not yet have full Roman citizenship.

In the Imperial period a legion was usually commanded by a legate who was a senator or equestrian, but in the late Republic the legion lacked a permanent commander. Instead, the provincial governor appointed senators from his staff to command one or more legions. These might be legates of quite senior status (Caesar's most experienced legate, Labienus, had held the important magistracy of Praetor), or they might be much younger men like Publius Crassus who was just beginning his senatorial career. Each legion had six military tribunes who were usually equestrians or the sons of senators gaining military experience before starting their own political careers. Making such appointments allowed Caesar to repay debts of patronage and enhance his own base of influential friends and clients for the future.

Perhaps the most important officers within the legion were the centurions, 60 in each legion. Appointed for their bravery and experience, these men were responsible for the training of their centuries and the day-to-day running of the legion whether on campaign or in winter quarters. Although some legions might be kept under arms for extended periods of time, in the late Republic they were not permanent entities and so the centurions provided a vital continuity of knowledge and experience as new legions were raised for campaigns like Caesar's. Centurions were the backbone of the legion and in combat they were expected to show leadership and courage. Unusually for Roman histories, Caesar regularly name-checks his centurions who excel in these qualities, but he also blames them when things go wrong, criticising his centurions for over-eagerness at Gergovia as well as those who led their men into difficulties through their desire to gain plaudits and military decorations for a successful action. The senior centurions of each legion (the *primi ordines*) regularly attended Caesar's councils of war and

Tombstone of Titus Calidius Severus, centurion of Legion XV Apollinaris from Carnuntum on the Danube with transverse crest distinctive to centurions. (Photo By DEA / A. DAGLI ORTI/De Agostini via Getty Images)

would have contributed to strategic discussions. There was considerable competition for these high-ranking positions, as Caesar notes when he recounts the rivalry between the two centurions of a legion which may be the Eleventh, Pullo and Vorenus, during the attack on Quintus Cicero's camp in the winter of 55 BC. Both were vying to be promoted to primus pilus, the senior centurion of the legion, and each tried to outdo the other in bravery but ended up saving the other's life.

Legionaries were armed at state expense, and were well equipped for their military roles. Each legionary, with his mail coat and bronze or iron helmet, was armed as well as the most wealthy and successful Celtic warriors and this must have given them a huge psychological advantage when facing the Gauls. The large shield or *scutum* provided additional protection. The legionary's principal weapons were the *pilum*

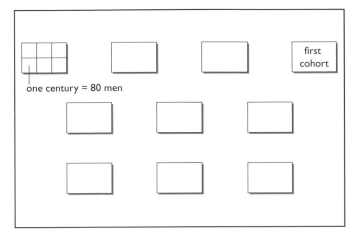

one century = 80 men

first cohort

The Roman legion was arranged into ten cohorts of six centuries. The cohort of c. 480 men was a key tactical unit in the Roman army and provided great flexibility as one or more cohorts could be detached from a legion for tactical purposes.

(javelin) and short sword, the *gladius*. Equipment was not uniform as in modern armies, and Caesar's soldiers would have decorated their kit according to preference and funds: the biographer Suetonius claims that by the civil war that followed the conquest of Gaul, the weapons Caesar's soldiers used were inlaid with gold and silver. Personalised equipment meant soldiers were more visible on the battlefield and could be identified and rewarded for their bravery. Centurions too were more visible because of the transverse crests they wore on their helmets; this helped their soldiers see them more easily in the confusion of battle, but also made them targets for the enemy.

Recruitment to the legions was based on a mixture of conscription and volunteering, the only qualification for service being citizenship, at least in theory. Recruits were supposed to be at least 17, although the majority were in their early 20s when they joined up. Roman ideology preferred recruits from rural backgrounds rather than from towns and cities with their perceived softening and corrupting influences, but Caesar probably experienced little difficulty in raising troops for his campaigns in Gaul because there had previously been little wide-scale recruitment in Cisalpine Gaul. The legionaries signed up for military service of no fixed length, although they could expect to be

discharged with a grant of land on which to settle after five years or so continuous service. Military pay was not especially good, but there were plenty of opportunities for enrichment, particularly on a lucrative campaign like Caesar's conquest of Gaul with the likelihood of generous amounts of booty.

While the legions were armed and equipped uniformly, and were principally heavy infantry, the variation in type of forces a successful army needed was provided by auxiliary units raised from other provinces of the Roman empire or from neighbouring states and tribes friendly to Rome. It was up to the provincial governor to maintain friendly relationships established by his predecessors with local tribes, such as the treaty of friendship between Rome and the Aedui. Caesar was so successful in his early campaigns in Gaul and his military prestige so great that he was able to attract auxiliary units from the Germans as well as support from Gallic tribes. These provided him with another source of cavalry that was particularly valuable when the loyalty of the Aedui wavered in 52 BC. Auxiliaries used their own fighting techniques, they were not trained in the Roman style of fighting, and they were commanded by their own officers, usually members of the ruling elite of the tribe or state from which they were recruited.

Gallic and Germanic tribal elites provided the majority of Caesar's cavalry, though these were not always reliable or effective and sometimes lacked discipline, particularly early on in the campaigns. The auxiliary cavalry suffered a drubbing at the hands of the Nervian cavalry in 57 BC but by the end of the campaigns this cavalry had become a powerful force that contributed to Caesar's victory in the Civil War. The German cavalry sometimes worked in concert with light infantry, which allowed the holding of terrain in addition to the useful mobility of cavalry.

Whilst saddles in the ancient world lacked stirrups, the horned design of the Celtic saddle meant that cavalry could act as shock troops and be highly effective, and it seems likely that the majority of cavalry

OPPOSITE
Mid-1st-century AD column base from Mainz, Germany showing legionaries in combat. (Photo By DEA PICTURE LIBRARY/De Agostini via Getty Images)

A 1st-century BC relief from Ascoli with slingers in action. Both sides in the Gallic war used slingers to great effect. (Photo By DEA / A. DAGLI ORTI/De Agostini via Getty Images)

fighting in the Gallic war on both sides were using such saddles. Cavalry troops might vary considerably in their equipment, since they equipped themselves, but a wealthy cavalryman might have a mail shirt and helmet, an oval or hexagonal shield which was more manoeuvrable on horseback than a rectangular one, a spear and a long sword, which was ideal for running down those fleeing from battle, one of the principal roles of the cavalry.

The Roman army in Gaul included slingers from the Balearics and archers from Crete and Numidia who

provided lightly armed mobile troops to increase the firepower of the army, particularly at a distance or in a siege. Their role is rarely commented upon, but they added an important degree of flexibility to the Roman army. Additional infantry was provided by Gallic tribes in the same way as cavalry, and would have consisted of groups of warriors from tribes who were allied to Rome, like the Aedui, or who swiftly surrendered to Caesar following his invasion, like the Remi. The wealthiest of these warriors were probably armed and equipped in a way very similar to the Roman legionaries, but the

Gauls placed greater emphasis on individual prowess and prominent displays of courage in battle, rather than the discipline and training of the legions.

Roman logistical support was generally well organised, with a supply system usually reliant on shuttling provisions from a supply base to the campaigning army. The army made use of Gaul's navigable rivers to move supplies around, but the limited road system and the speed of Caesar's movements led to difficulties. Although Caesar could call on his Gallic allies and later the subjected tribes for supplies, his movements and the direction of the campaign were often heavily influenced by logistical demands. An understanding of this lay behind the Gallic scorched-earth policy in the revolt of 52 BC. When the legions were in winter quarters, Caesar ensured they were garrisoned in the territories of recently conquered tribes to serve the dual purpose of ensuring a strong military presence in newly reduced territory, and punishing those who resisted Rome by forcing them to feed the occupying army, a penalty that could have affected a tribe's ability to support its own population. The winter allowed troops time to recover from the often exhaustive campaigning that Caesar demanded of his armies, in particular those who were sick or had been wounded in fighting. Roman imperial armies had medics attached to them, and this may have been the case in the late Republic, too. In the aftermath of pitched battle Roman armies usually paused, sometimes for several days, so the dead could be buried and the wounded treated. The wounded would later be escorted to a base, probably a supply base, to recuperate before rejoining their units.

Gauls, Britons and Germans

In the 1st century BC Celtic tribes employed different methods of warfare. Although prowess in combat remained important for the tribal elite, in some tribes, particularly in southern and central Gaul, other means were becoming available to gain and maintain status. The Aeduan aristocrat Dumnorix fought as a cavalryman to display his elite warrior status, but he also held a monopoly over the wine trade, which enhanced his wealth and therefore his position within Celtic society. Somewhat paradoxically, the Romans interpreted the spread of Mediterranean culture into northern Europe as a demoralising factor. Caesar perceived the Belgae as the bravest of the Gauls 'because they are furthest away from the culture and civilisation of Provence, and are least often visited by merchants importing degenerate luxury goods, and also because they are nearest to the Germans who live across the Rhine and with whom they are continuously at war'.

In most Gallic tribes, raiding neighbours was the warrior's principal means of acquiring wealth and position, and tribes sought to extend their influence over less powerful neighbours. The most secure were those with wide influence and many dependent tribes. Tribes might form alliances with neighbours or even, in the case of the Sequani, the Germans, in order to increase their own military prowess and security. Gallic war bands consisted of groups of warriors belonging to an elite class following their chieftain and concentrating on raiding; larger-scale armies of the kind faced by the Romans in Gaul were probably less common, and probably included dependent farmers who may not normally have been involved in regular warfare. If Caesar really did face an army of 50,000 Helvetii and their allies, it probably included tribesmen of all statuses, but we hear no details of them or how they were armed and equipped. The warriors equipped themselves according to their wealth and status: the braver and more successful, the more likely they were to be able to adorn themselves with beautifully decorated and high quality equipment.

Many warriors would probably have possessed mail coats and may have had defensive equipment quite similar to a Roman legionary, with the mail armour providing reasonably good protection from the slashing blows of the long Celtic swords, a bronze or iron helmet, and a sword and shield. Stylistically Gallic helmets were

very similar to some Roman helmets; indeed the *coolus* helmet which evolved into one of the main helmets of the Roman imperial army was originally a Gallic design of high quality reflecting the technological skills of Gallic blacksmithing. Gallic warriors carried spears and swords, the latter considerably longer than the Roman *gladius*. They were designed primarily for slashing rather than stabbing, and pointed to a fighting technique that required plenty of room for the individual to wield his long weapon. Though the Greek historian Polybius claims these long swords had a tendency to bend on impact, many were made of high quality iron and they were extremely effective weapons. The elongated Gallic rectangular shield was probably made of hide or wood like the Roman *scutum*. Some shields may not have been

particularly thick or strong, which may explain why Caesar reports that the Roman *pila* were able to pierce several of them simultaneously; the bronze shields that survive from antiquity may have been for decorative or ceremonial purposes and not actually for use in battle. Given that some fighters probably lacked body armour, and indeed some may have chosen to fight without armour to stress their courage and military prowess, the shield was a vital piece of protective equipment. When their shields were put out of action by the Roman *pila*, the Helvetii became dangerously exposed to the Roman attack.

Celtic cavalry, manned by the wealthiest warriors, was particularly effective and scored significant victories against Caesar's more numerous auxiliary cavalry in the

first couple of campaigning seasons. The lack of stirrups was no bar to powerful cavalry: the design of the Celtic saddle provided its rider with a secure mount from which to throw spears, thrust with a spear or slash with a sword and implement shock tactics. Some German cavalry may have used these saddles as well, and their horsemanship and co-operation with the light infantry who regularly worked alongside them was clearly impressive and shows levels of training by the German tribes that we hear little about in any sources. The Celtic tribes in Britain were still using chariots, something that had gone out of fashion on the Continent, but their speed and agility and the novelty of them caused the Roman infantry difficulties. The chariots served as battlefield 'taxis' for the wealthiest nobles, dropping them off at the fighting and then collecting them up again if they were injured or needed to withdraw from the battle.

Firepower was available in the form of slingers and archers, although these men were probably not members of the warrior class as this form of warfare was not really regarded as 'heroic'. Slingers were sometimes involved in open warfare (such as the Gallic ambush of a Roman column in 54 BC), but more often in the defence of hill forts, along with archers. In preparation for the general revolt of 52 BC, Vercingetorix called up all the archers of Gaul; they were probably Gauls of the lower classes, but were vital to the success of the strategy of the revolt.

ABOVE
Silver *denarius* of 118 BC. Head of Roma (obverse); Celtic warrior in chariot hurling spear (reverse). (Photo by Heritage Art/ Heritage Images via Getty Images)

OPPOSITE
A 1st-century BC sculpture of a Gallic warrior. Elite Gallic warriors and Roman soldiers were similarly equipped, with mail armour, sword and large shield. (Photo By DEA / A. DAGLI ORTI/De Agostini via Getty Images)

Very little is known about the organisation of Gallic armies and their workings in pitched battle. Although there seems to have been a reliance on infantry and cavalry charges at the start of battles to break the enemy lines, the tactics of the Helvetii in 58 BC show effective battle planning and use of reserves. Pitched battle, even at a small scale, provided one of the best opportunities to display military prowess and so was an important way of making war, but not all Gallic tribes were so keen on meeting the enemy in the open, especially when that enemy was as powerful as Rome, so the military strategies of the tribes the Romans encountered varied. While some stronger tribes and coalitions like the Nervii were eager to meet the Romans in pitched battle, others, like the tribes of Aquitania in south-western Gaul, relied more on hit-and-run tactics and attacking the invaders' supply lines as Vercingetorix planned to do during the revolt of 52 BC. Some of the coastal tribes who possessed mobile wealth (usually in the form of cattle) were able to withdraw into marshlands and avoid direct conflict with the Romans, like the Menapii and Morini of the Channel coast. The Veneti, whose wealth was founded on trade and whose military strength was maritime, based their strategy around defence of hill forts situated on coastal promontories, simply moving by sea to another when one was about to be captured by the Romans. Different tribes, then, had the military capacity to adapt their strategies to deal with the new threat of Rome, and some of these variations were quite successful in impeding Roman progress. Hit-and-run tactics and the avoidance of pitched battle may also have been preferred by Gallic tribes, or necessitated by the absence of the kind of logistical support that Roman armies could depend upon. Large Gallic armies could not remain in existence for very long and unless a decisive engagement quickly occurred such an army might have to disband because of lack of supplies. The Belgic army in 57 BC, which combined many different tribes, was forced to dissipate for this reason when a decisive engagement with Caesar was not forthcoming.

The professional Roman army had many advantages over the armies of the Gallic warrior societies and it was not surprising that several tribes quickly went over to Rome, or that under the leadership of such an effective general as Caesar, the initial conquest of Gaul was completed remarkably quickly.

Gallic flair and Roman discipline

Gallic and Roman fighting styles were quite different. For both cultures, victory in pitched battle was the ultimate accolade for a warrior or soldier, and also for tribal chieftains and Roman generals. To show courage on the battlefield was expected; to die in battle was glorious. By the mid-1st century BC, when Caesar began his conquest of Gaul, Romans and Gauls had been fighting each other on and off for centuries. In their literature the Romans betrayed both a fear of their 'barbarian' neighbours, and a sneaking admiration for the way they fought. Gauls were perceived as taller than Romans (they are portrayed as being of almost giant stature in some accounts); certainly they probably were generally a little taller than the average Italian legionary, and the Romans seem to have been rather defensive about being shorter than their adversaries. Nonetheless, the style of fighting they employed was perfect for fighting Gauls. Indeed, the organisation of legions into maniples (120-man units), and the introduction of the large *scutum* and short *gladius* as the principal weapons of legionary hand-to-hand combat may have been developed as a result of conflicts with the Gauls in the 4th century BC.

The Gallic fighting style allowed the warrior to display himself on the battlefield, either through fighting naked or by wearing elaborately decorated armour, and he showed off his valour by fighting

Silver *denarius* issued by Julius Caesar depicting a trophy celebrating a victory over the Gauls. (Photo By DEA / A. RIZZI/De Agostini via Getty Images)

as an individual. The warrior's long sword required him to have a fair amount of space around him on the battlefield in order to operate properly. The Celtic sword was essentially a slashing weapon and in the hands of a tall Gallic warrior with a long reach, could be a deadly blade, particularly against shorter opposition with short swords. But the Gallic warriors did not operate with the same disciplined coherence as Roman legions; though training and experience must have provided them with an understanding of tactics, and commands could have been communicated on the battlefield through musical instruments, they did not possess the same degree of training to fight as a unit that Roman soldiers did. When forced to retreat, they could not always maintain ranks and withdraw in good order, something that required considerable training and trust in one's fellow soldiers. This made them vulnerable to outflanking manoeuvres and to cavalry attacks on retreating warriors. Lack of space to swing their swords could also cause havoc in the Gallic ranks. When forced together, Gallic warriors might struggle to use their swords effectively, and this made them vulnerable to an enemy who could operate at very close quarters with deadly efficiency.

The Roman legionary's equipment did not make him reliant on his neighbour's shield for protection in combat as in a Greek phalanx formation. He fought as an individual, but he was dependent on the strength of his unit. If his comrades in his century, cohort or legion gave way, he would eventually become exposed to attack on the flank or rear. The success of the Roman army lay in the strength of its formations, and that was based on unit morale, discipline and training. These can clearly be seen when Caesar's legions came under sudden attack by the Nervii in the second season of campaigning. The legionaries did not even need their officers to give them orders: they automatically dropped their entrenching tools, picked up their weapons, and formed a battle line. Their training ensured that even though they were not with their own units and the

men they normally fought with, they were resourceful enough to create an effective line of battle. Roman soldiers were not automatons in a 'military machine': they were trained to think and use their initiative as well as follow orders. The training and discipline instilled in the soldiers meant that Roman units could move over battlefields in formation and even retreat while maintaining a defensive formation, an invaluable technique in warfare for minimising casualties.

In combat with their taller Gallic opponents with their slashing swords, they threw their *pila* and then moved in very close for hand-to-hand combat. The large *scutum* protected most of the legionary's front and left side, his short *gladius* was ideal for stabbing in close-quarters fighting, and he could even punch at the enemy with the metal boss of his shield. If the legionaries moved in close enough, they could literally cramp the style of their Gallic opponents while still giving themselves the small amount of room they needed to operate effectively. The short *gladius* was a brutally efficient tool for killing: a short stab at the

Roman triumphal arch in Orange, early 1st century AD, depicting battle between Gauls and Romans. (Photo By DEA / S. VANNINI/ De Agostini via Getty Images)

torso or especially the belly of his opponent, who may have been fighting without armour, and he would have been killed or badly injured with damage to internal organs and serious bleeding. Though Roman soldiers were trained to stab with their swords, that did not stop them from slashing with them, and the fine quality and perfect weighting of the *gladius* meant that they could easily hack off limbs. The average Roman legionary may have been shorter in stature than his Gallic opponent, but his equipment meant he was not at a disadvantage. Moreover, the tactics and fighting style employed in pitched battle against Celtic opponents turned it into an advantage. Usually, in pitched battle Roman discipline triumphed over Gallic flair.

OUTBREAK
The migration of the Helvetii

On 28 March 58 BC the Celtic tribe of the Helvetii left their homes in Switzerland and, along with their neighbours, the Raurici, Tulingi, Latobrigi and Boii, began a migration west. The purpose of this mass movement of tribes, including women, children and livestock, was to move to western Gaul, to the lands of other Gallic tribes on which they intended to settle after defeating the inhabitants and forcing them to move on. These mass migrations of whole tribes were not unheard of, and a similar movement of German tribes in the late 2nd century BC had led to the clashes between them and Rome and the catastrophic defeats of several Roman armies. The migration of the Helvetii did not come as a surprise to anyone, however, as extensive planning had been observed. Preparations had begun three years previously. By the late 60s BC the Helvetii were feeling the pressure of space. Hemmed in by the mountains of Switzerland, they had little opportunity to expand their territory to cater for a growing population and they were also concerned at the presence to the north of their land of German tribes which had been migrating westwards, particularly the aggressive Suebic king Ariovistus who had settled in the territory of the Sequani after they and the Arverni had sought his support in local wars with the Aedui.

The Helvetii had begun their preparations in 61 BC, building up three years' supply of grain for the journey and for sowing the new lands they planned to take over in western Gaul. Other supplies were gathered, draught animals and wagons. Much of this was done under the leadership of a Helvetian noble, Orgetorix, who also secretly formed an alliance with two Gallic aristocrats, Casticus of the Sequani and Dumnorix the Aeduan, whose brother Diviciacus had close ties with Rome. The three seem to have planned to seize power in their tribes and lead a coalition, perhaps to conquer and partition Gaul between the three tribes or, more likely, to tackle the dual threats of the Germans under Ariovistus and the increasing threat of Roman intervention or invasion. Whatever the purpose of the plot, it was discovered and Orgetorix committed suicide before he could be put on trial for conspiring to make himself king. This did not deter the Helvetii from their migration plans, however; in the spring of 58 BC they burned their towns, villages and surplus grain to rule out the possibility of abandoning the migration, and with thousands of wagons started west towards the Gallic lands west of the Rhône, and towards the Roman province.

Gauls and Romans were concerned by the prospect of the migration. The movement of several thousand people would cause huge damage to the lands they passed through and could destabilise the whole of southern Gaul as tribes chose whether to join the Helvetii in a bid for land or to oppose them. At the end of their migration the Helvetii planned to seize land from other tribes, causing further disruption to the political balance of the area. Some tribes would have looked towards Rome for assistance, and in 60 BC the Senate had sent ambassadors to Gallic tribes in an attempt to discourage them from joining the Helvetii. The proposed migration threatened the security of Rome's allies including the Aedui and the Allobroges, as well as Provence with its desirable fertile lands. While it was unlikely that the Helvetii would have turned south to threaten Italy, memories of the disasters inflicted by the Germans may have made Rome nervous

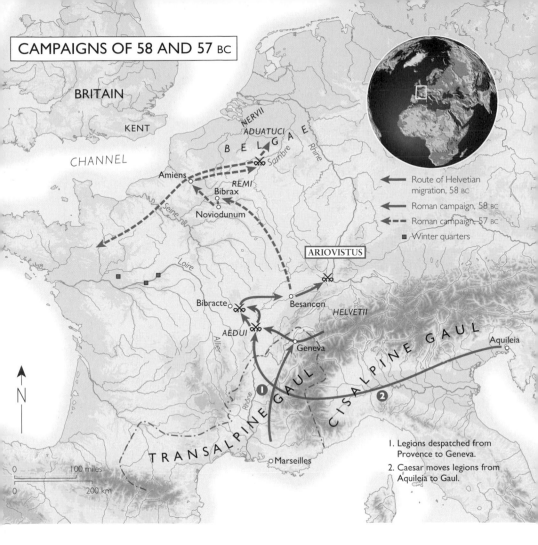

CAMPAIGNS OF 58 AND 57 BC

BRITAIN

KENT

CHANNEL

NERVII

ADUATUCI

BELGAE

Sambre

Rhine

Amiens

REMI

Bibrax

Noviodunum

Seine

ARIOVISTUS

Loire

Bibracte

Besancon

HELVETII

AEDUI

Allier

Geneva

CISALPINE GAUL

Aquileia

Rhone

TRANSALPINE GAUL

CISALPINE GAUL

Marseilles

→ Route of Helvetian migration, 58 BC

→ Roman campaign, 58 BC

⇢ Roman campaign, 57 BC

■ Winter quarters

N

1. Legions despatched from Provence to Geneva.
2. Caesar moves legions from Aquileia to Gaul.

| 0 | 100 miles |
| 0 | 200 km |

about migratory tribes, and there was a real worry over Germanic tribes moving into the vacated Helvetian lands. In Roman thought, Germans were less desirable neighbours than Gauls. Rome did not want upheavals on its northern borders, and the preparations for the migrations led to thoughts of war in Rome. Ostensibly launched to protect Rome's interests, a war against the Helvetii would probably have led to the greater Roman intervention in Gaul that concerned Orgetorix and his allies.

A Roman war in Gaul was becoming increasingly inevitable by the late 60s. The consul of 60 BC,

Metellus, seems to have been very keen to campaign against the Gauls and obtain a triumph. The leading Roman politician Marcus Cicero describes him as 'not over-happy at the reports of peace in Gaul', after Orgetorix's failed coup, and the consul of 59 BC, Julius Caesar, was equally eager to make his mark militarily. The threat posed by the Helvetii to Provence and Gallic allies provided the *casus belli* and the opportunity for Caesar to involve himself in Gaul, but had this not arisen, he may well have found some other excuse to campaign there. As it was, once the Helvetian threat had been neutralised, he swiftly found justifications to move deeper into Gaul and Gallic affairs to ensure sensational victories and conquests. These were easily found in the request by Rome's Aeduan allies for assistance against the threats posed by both Ariovistus and the migrating Helvetii, and from there the Roman conquest of Gaul was Caesar's most likely aim. When Caesar, the new governor of Illyricum, Cisalpine and Transalpine Gaul, heard that the Helvetii were finally on the move, it was his duty to protect his province of Transalpine Gaul, which was directly in the path of the migrants. The Helvetii asked Caesar for permission to cross Roman territory and when he refused they turned north to continue their migration without trespassing on the Roman land. Although they were now no longer a direct threat to Rome, Caesar followed them and made an unprovoked attack on the Helvetii while they were crossing a river. The actions of the Helvetii were sufficient to a Roman audience to warrant such a reaction, especially since the Romans considered them to be 'barbarians'. The Roman conquest of Gaul was an aggressive war of expansion led by a general who was seeking to advance his career and standing amongst his peers, but who was acting within the expectations of Roman society and its value systems.

THE FIGHTING
Invasion, siege and conquest

58 BC: The first campaign

In the first year of his governorship, Caesar fought and won two major pitched battles and set himself up to conquer Gaul. The speed and decisiveness with which he operated must have impressed his political rivals in Rome and terrified the Gauls. Caesar had freed them from the menace of the migrating Helvetii and the German king Ariovistus, but now he threatened their independence himself.

Caesar was still in Rome when news arrived in mid-March that the Helvetii were on the move, heading west towards Geneva and southern Gaul, dangerously close to the Roman province. He immediately headed for Provence, ordering the only legion stationed there to make for Geneva and to destroy the bridge over the Rhône. He levied auxiliary troops in Provence and raised two new legions in northern Italy. Playing for time, he agreed to consider a request that the Helvetii be allowed to pass, but then refused once his troops had built defences – a 19-mile-long defended rampart – that forced the Helvetii away from Roman territory and into central France. He then dashed back to Italy to collect the two new legions and three veteran legions in garrison at Aquileia, marched them through the Alps in early summer and caught up with the Helvetii as they were crossing the Saône. Three-quarters had crossed, but Caesar attacked those remaining. Some escaped into the woods, but his legions slaughtered the rest, a sign of the brutalities that were to come. The casualty figures are not recorded.

Crossing the Saône in a single day on pontoons, Caesar caught up with the main body of Helvetii and trailed them at a discreet distance as they travelled away from the river, refusing to be drawn into combat except on his terms. The Helvetii were keen to avoid battle and tried to negotiate, but Caesar's demands were too severe, perhaps intentionally since he was probably eager to fight when the tactical situation became favourable. It did a few days later and a force under Labienus took the high ground above the Helvetian camp in preparation for an attack, but a veteran scout panicked and wrongly reported to Caesar that the flashes of arms he had seen on the hill were definitely Gallic, not Roman, so the attack had to be aborted.

Caesar continued to tail the Helvetii but was finally forced towards Bibracte to collect supplies from his Aeduan allies, his own supply train being stuck on the Saône. Perhaps hoping to cut the Romans off from their supplies, the Helvetii decided to give battle and attacked the Roman rearguard. Caesar deployed on a slope under cover of a cavalry screen and pitched battle followed.

Battle against the Helvetii

There are no figures for the size of the Helvetian army. Their allies, the Boii and Tulingi, numbered *c.* 15,000 according to Caesar, but the reporting of enemy numbers in antiquity was notoriously unreliable and Caesar is no exception; it is unlikely that the total Gallic army was more than *c.* 50,000 men. The Helvetii formed up in very close order. They gathered their baggage, wagons and families beyond the left wing of their battle line along with their allies, the Boii and Tulingi.

The Roman forces consisted of six legions numbering *c.* 24,000–30,000 men, as well as unknown numbers of auxiliary infantry and cavalry. Two of the legions

BATTLE AGAINST THE HELVETII, 58 BC

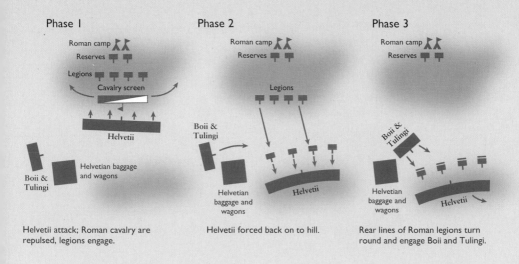

Phase 1

Roman camp
Reserves
Legions
Cavalry screen
Helvetii
Boii & Tulingi
Helvetian baggage and wagons

Helvetii attack; Roman cavalry are repulsed, legions engage.

Phase 2

Roman camp
Reserves
Legions
Boii & Tulingi
Helvetian baggage and wagons
Helvetii

Helvetii forced back on to hill.

Phase 3

Roman camp
Reserves
Boii & Tulingi
Helvetian baggage and wagons
Helvetii

Rear lines of Roman legions turn round and engage Boii and Tulingi.

were newly recruited and many of the auxiliaries were Gauls and Caesar was probably unsure of their fighting capabilities. He deployed these forces on the high ground as a reserve and to guard the Roman encampment; he fought the battle with just his four veteran legions which he deployed as a *triplex acies* on ground sloping down towards the Helvetii. (Four cohorts were in the front line, with two further lines of three cohorts each as a reserve force.)

The first attack of the Helvetii was easily repulsed by the Romans, who had the advantage of the slope and superior weaponry in the form of their *pila,* which stuck into the enemy's shields, weighing them down and pinning them together. The Helvetii were forced back, but their attack may have been a feint. As the Roman cohorts followed the retreating Helvetii, the Boii and Tulingi outflanked the Roman right, leaving it dangerously exposed. At this point the Helvetii renewed the fight and the Romans were surrounded.

Close-quarters infantry combat ensued. The brilliant tactical flexibility of the legion enabled Caesar to order the rear line of cohorts to turn round. The legions fought the battle on two fronts and the Roman reserves guarding the camp on the hill were not even engaged. Nonetheless it was a hard-fought battle and Caesar notes the bravery of the enemy fighters who stood their ground for hours. Eventually, though, the Helvetii were forced to flee and the Boii and Tulingi were forced back against the wagons and slaughtered along with the women and children.

Caesar was unable to give pursuit immediately because of the damage done to his own army. Instead he rested for three days to see to his wounded before continuing his pursuit of the Helvetii, who promptly surrendered. Concerned that Germanic tribes might move into the lands vacated by the Helvetii, Caesar demanded hostages and the surrender of weapons and escaped Roman slaves and ordered the survivors home. He claims that of the 368,000 who set out on the migration, only 110,000 returned.

After dealing with the Helvetii, Caesar turned on the German tribes who had occupied land on the western bank of the Rhine under their king Ariovistus. Caesar needed a good reason for attacking a king who was a 'Friend and Ally of the Roman People', but requests for help from the Aedui who were also allied to Rome and from other Gallic tribes threatened by the German presence were sufficient. Both sides aimed to occupy the strategically important town of Besançon but Caesar got there first. Here fear spread through Caesar's inexperienced troops and even among some of his officers that Ariovistus and his army were going to be a much tougher prospect than the migrating tribes the Romans had comprehensively defeated. Caesar had to restore discipline by threatening to march off with only one of his legions. When he did march, with all his army, the two leaders met to parley but neither was prepared to damage his reputation by backing down and agreeing to the other's demands to vacate Gaul. Pitched battle was inevitable, although Caesar was the more eager to force

an engagement, perhaps because of his usual difficulties with his supplies. He was dependent for supplies on Gallic tribes whose reliability was sometimes suspect, and the speed with which he liked to operate on campaign only added to the uncertainties of his supply lines. Eventually the Romans forced Ariovistus to deploy by marching in battle formation right at the German encampment.

The Germans parked their wagons behind their battle line, Caesar claims to prevent the warriors escaping, but it was more likely to prevent an outflanking manoeuvre by the Romans. The engagement began with both the Germans and the Romans charging so quickly that the Romans had no space to throw their *pila*, and an intense period of hand-to-hand combat ensued. The German left was routed by the Roman right under the personal command of Caesar, but the Roman left was coming under pressure. The officer in command of the

Roman soldiers foraging, Trajan's Column, 2nd century AD. Foraging was an important supplement to the Roman logistical system. (Photo By DEA / A. DAGLI ORTI/De Agostini via Getty Images)

cavalry, Publius Crassus, saw this and had the initiative to redeploy the third line of each legion to attack the German right. Again it was the flexibility of legionary tactics that turned the battle and the Germans fled, pursued the full five miles to the Rhine during which the majority of German casualties would have been inflicted. The German losses are reported at 80,000 and the battle was clearly an outright victory for the Romans. In just one year Caesar was able to report to his rivals in Rome that he had defeated two of Rome's traditional and most feared enemies, Gauls and Germans. He wintered his legions near Vesontio and returned to northern Italy to attend to the civil aspects of his governorship.

German cavalry tactics

Although the horses the German cavalrymen used were small and sometimes of poor quality, the cavalry itself was made particularly effective through the addition of a force of light infantry that worked in tandem with the cavalry. This provided the manoeuvrability of cavalry along with the staying power of infantry.

With the six thousand cavalry was the same number of infantry, the swiftest and bravest men, each chosen from the whole army by a cavalryman for his own protection; they went into battle together. The cavalry would fall back on them; if the cavalry were in difficulties the infantry ran to help; if a cavalryman had been wounded and fallen from his horse, they surrounded him. They had become so swift through training that on a long advance or a quick retreat they could keep up by running, holding on to the horses' manes.

- Caesar, *Gallic War*

57 BC: Conquest of the east

By early 57 BC, if he had not already resolved to do so the previous year, Caesar had decided to conquer the whole of Gaul. Some Gallic tribes were persuaded to form alliances with Rome because of the protection and influence such a relationship would bring within Gaul, and they may have felt, probably correctly, that as conquest was inevitable, it was better to be on the winning side. The Aedui in central Gaul were encouraged to remain Caesar's staunchest allies by his willingness to let them expand their influence over defeated Gallic tribes. The Remi in northern Gaul preferred to fight with Rome rather than against it and like the Aedui remained loyal to Caesar and Rome throughout the campaigns, providing valuable intelligence to the Romans. However, the majority of Belgic tribes feared Rome's growing power in the region and prepared to resist, soliciting help from the Germans. Caesar lists the different Belgic tribes resisting him at the start of the year's fighting and claims they could muster an army of 200,000 warriors, though this is very likely an exaggeration to stress his achievements in defeating them.

Caesar raised two more legions, bringing the total to eight (32,000–40,000 men, plus auxiliaries), and at the start of the campaigning season headed for northern Gaul. His intention was to defeat the powerful Belgic tribes and cut them off from German support to the east. The Belgae caught up with him near Bibrax and tried to capture the *oppidum* from the occupying Remi. Caesar despatched Numidian and Cretan archers along with slingers from the Balearics from his auxiliary forces to support the defence of the town and demonstrate the strength of his support for the Remi. Unable to capture the town, the Belgae instead ravaged the land and then turned towards Caesar's camp by the river Aisne. Caesar had prepared for a pitched battle on ground very favourable to his army, entrenching camp on rising ground and extending two of the ramparts by means of trenches to well-defended redoubts bristling with artillery. These extensions to the camp ramparts were to prevent a Belgic outflanking manoeuvre should battle ensue and show that even if the numbers of Belgic warriors were over-estimated, they still outnumbered the Romans to the point that Caesar was nervous of being outflanked. However, the Roman position had been so strongly prepared that the expected pitched battle did not ensue: the Belgae were not going to accept a major

engagement under such disadvantageous conditions. Nonetheless there was fierce engagement between the Belgae and Caesar's forces as the former attempted to force a crossing of the river and attack the Roman position by a different route and cut them off from their supplies. Roman firepower was decisive and helped to drive back the Belgic warriors, with the cavalry despatching those who did get across the river.

This reverse and concerns about supplies led to a resolution of sorts. The Belgae too were running short of supplies, and without the logistical support that the Romans had access to, they simply disbanded their army with the intention of re-forming it if, or when, Caesar threatened them directly. Although Caesar presents these engagements as a win for Rome, the Belgic tribes had not been yet been subjected.

Caesar's officers

Caesar had under his command a number of officers who were also senators in Rome and whom he could appoint to senior positions. A quaestor was attached to the province of Gaul and had some financial responsibilities, and as a junior senator could also command troops, sometimes independently. Publius Crassus seems to have been a particularly able young man who held this role but in 54 BC he went to join his father on the doomed campaign against the Parthians; he was killed at Carrhae the following year.

Caesar was also allowed to appoint a number of legates, usually more senior senators like Labienus who had held the Praetorship, a senior magistracy in Rome. These men could be placed in command of quite large forces of several legions plus cavalry, and trusted with independent commands. Labienus was left in charge of the entire province of Gaul during the expeditions to Britain. Appointing legates provided an opportunity to pay back political debts or to place others in your debt through patronage, although his debt to Caesar did not prevent Labienus from siding with Pompey in the Civil War.

The speed at which Roman armies could move proved an important factor in the success of the year's campaigns. Caesar pounced on the *oppidum* of the Suessiones at Noviodunum (on the river Aisne), hoping to capture it before the warriors returned after the Belgic army had disbanded. Though the warriors were able to sneak in at night, they quickly surrendered when they saw the siege preparations, roofed sheds and siege towers which allowed the Roman infantry to approach the *oppidum*'s walls under cover: clearly they had never experienced anything like Roman siege warfare before. The psychological effects of this surrender were widespread, with the Bellovaci and Ambiones surrendering to the Romans without resistance and handing over to the Romans their weapons and hostages. The next tribe though, the powerful Nervii, decided to resist, formed an alliance with the neighbouring Atrebates and Viromandui and planned to ambush Caesar's army as it was marching or at its most vulnerable when encamping. Making use of the terrain, land patched with dense woodland and divided by high hedgerows, the Nervii set an ambush in woods on the far side of the river Sambre. The Romans began fortifying camp on the near side of the river despite knowing that the enemy were close. Cavalry and light infantry were sent across the water to scout and keep the Nervii away while the legionaries completed the encampment, but they were easily repulsed by the Nervii, who then charged the entrenching Roman soldiers. Caesar had failed to deploy a screen of infantry to protect those entrenching, standard procedure when encamping in the presence of the enemy, and his legions were caught dispersed and unprepared. The two rookie legions forming the rearguard had not even arrived at the campsite.

Battle against the Nervii

Caesar had eight legions, two of which – the newly recruited units – were still marching, and an unknown number of auxiliary infantry and cavalry. His army may have numbered over 40,000, but he claims that the Nervii had at least 60,000 warriors of the Nervii, Atrebates and Viromandui.

BATTLE AGAINST THE NERVII, 57 BC

Phase 1

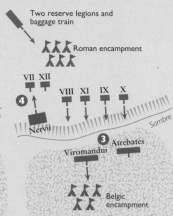

Phase 2

Phase 3

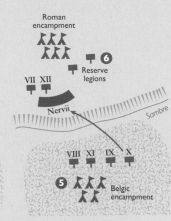

1. Roman cavalry and light infantry are repulsed.
2. Nervii, Viromandui and Atrebates advance against Roman legions.

3. Atrebates and Viromandui are repulsed.
4. Legions VII and XII come under intense pressure from Nervii; Roman encampment is captured.

5. Belgic encampment captured; Legion X sent back to assist Roman camp.
6. Reserve Roman legions arrive and together the five legions massacre the Nervii.

Faced with a sudden attack, the Roman legionaries did exactly the right thing. Both they and their officers had a year's more experience than when they had panicked in the face of Ariovistus the previous year, and their training and discipline kicked in. They grabbed arms and automatically created a line of battle, the soldiers forming up with the nearest standards rather than rushing around trying to find their own units and standards, an indication of good discipline and morale. There was no time for speeches in this very dynamic engagement and the fighting probably started piecemeal as different parts of the swiftly forming Roman lines came under attack. The IX and X legions held the left wing, the VIII and XI the centre, and the VII and XII the right wing.

The Nervii created a very strong left wing; the Viromandui held the centre and the Atrebates the right wing.

OPPOSITE
This 1st-century AD column base from Mainz, Germany shows captured 'barbarians' chained together to be sold into slavery. (Photo By DEA PICTURE LIBRARY/De Agostini via Getty Images)

The two cavalry forces were already engaged, with the Gallic cavalry mauling the Romans.

Despite the battle line being cut up by the hedgerows, the Romans held the line fast and withheld the onslaught from the Belgic tribes. The Roman centre was successful and the left wing repulsed the Atrebates, pursuing them across the Sambre. However, this success left the half-built Roman camp and the right wing of the battle line exposed, and the Gauls captured the camp.

Meanwhile, the Roman right wing was outflanked by the Nervii, several of the officers had been killed and the ranks had become too packed together to operate effectively; the situation was critical. Taking up a shield and a position on foot with the front rank soldiers, Caesar ordered the ranks opened up and the two legions to form a square so they could defend themselves from attack on all sides. His own presence helped to stiffen resistance until help arrived in the form of the X Legion, which Labienus, one of Caesar's most experienced legates, had sent back to assist after capturing the enemy encampment, and the two rookie legions of the rearguard which had finally arrived. The combined force of five legions turned the tide of battle and obliterated the Nervii who stood their ground until forced through huge casualties to surrender.

Caesar's over-confidence had led to a dangerous situation, but his personal bravery and leadership in a crisis situation, and the experience of his army and officers, turned it into a significant victory. This successful engagement broke the power of the Belgae to such an extent that even German tribes beyond the Rhine sent envoys to Caesar offering submission.

The Aduatuci, allies of the Nervii, withdrew into their hillfort and Caesar invested the site, preventing the defenders from escaping whilst his legions built siege equipment. At the novel sight of a wooden siege tower, the Aduatuci sent out emissaries to discuss terms. Caesar offered to spare the occupants provided they surrendered before the battering ram touched the walls of the *oppidum* – an important detail of the ancient

'rules' of war. The Aduatuci agreed, but then broke the terms of surrender and sortied under cover of darkness. The attack was repulsed, but Caesar waited until daylight before ordering the gates broken open. He claims that 53,000 prisoners were taken, all sold into slavery as an example of the consequences of breaking the terms of surrender; the profit from the sale was, by rights, Caesar's alone but he made sure that his soldiers benefitted too, an important means of cementing their loyalty to their commander.

In the latter half of the year Caesar sent his quaestor Crassus to campaign in the coastal areas of north-western Gaul. The claims of conquest were premature but the operations allowed the Romans to gather valuable intelligence and prepare for major campaigns in the area the following year; this almost certainly included preparations for naval warfare and the construction of ships, given the swiftness with which Roman ships were made available for the following year.

Towards winter, Caesar sent one of his senior officers, Galba, to open up the road over the Great St Bernard pass into Italy, allegedly for trade purposes. But he had been given an inadequate force of one under-strength legion and when Galba billeted his troops in the village of Octodurus he came under heavy attack from the local tribes who were concerned, probably rightly, that the Romans were more interested in conquest than trade routes. Galba's legion, the XII, was depleted after its mauling in battle with the Nervii and the poorly defended position they held was untenable. Galba was forced to abandon the campaign and break out, though according to reports they managed to kill some 10,000 Gauls on the way. Despite this setback, at the end of this second year, Caesar reported that Gaul was at peace, a gross over-exaggeration of the stability of the Roman gains after two campaigning seasons, and the Senate in Rome voted him an unprecedented 15-day public thanksgiving. This not only greatly increased Caesar's political and military reputation, but gave senatorial sanction to campaigning outside of his official province and tacit acceptance that the conquests would continue. He returned again to northern Italy to spend the winter; his legions were quartered in northern Gaul, the tribes there being forced to provide for the soldiers.

The Aedui

Friendly relations between Rome and the Aedui had existed since 122 BC, and Aeduan warriors had served as auxiliaries in Roman armies, particularly as cavalry. Their support was vital for Caesar's campaigns in Gaul: they provided additional forces, food supplies, and a friendly place to fall back on should the Romans suffer a reverse. They were able to pressurise some tribes into allying themselves to Rome, such as the Bellovaci in 57 BC, but there was not unanimous support for Rome amongst the tribe. While Diviciacus, an influential aristocrat who had been chief magistrate of the Aedui, was a staunch supporter of Rome, his brother Dumnorix was just as passionately opposed to the alliance and though he was killed by Roman troops in 54 BC, some anti-Roman sentiment continued. Some Aeduan forces joined the revolt of 52 BC, but the tribe's involvement was by no means total. In return for Aeduan support, Caesar had allowed the tribe to extend its influence, letting them settle the Boii on their territory after their defeat with the Helvetii, for example, and picking them out as one of only two tribes spared punishment after the surrender of Alesia. Their favoured status and the willingness with which they embraced Roman culture resulted in the Aedui producing the first Gallic senator after the emperor Claudius admitted Gauls to that institution.

56 BC: Naval warfare and the conquest of the west

Gallic resentment at the compulsion to feed the Roman legions over the winter showed itself when the Venetic tribes in north-western Gaul detained Roman officers sent out to procure grain and other supplies. Roman prestige demanded a forceful response. Since the Veneti were essentially a maritime force, ships were requisitioned from Gallic allies, warships constructed on the Loire, and oarsmen recruited in Provence with a view to beginning the naval campaign as early as the weather permitted. The Veneti knew that the capture of Roman officers would bring the invading army down on them and also

Trajan's Column, early 2nd century AD. Roman triremes operating in the Adriatic. (Photo By DEA / A. DAGLI ORTI/De Agostini via Getty Images)

prepared. They had the advantage of knowledge of both the land and the sea: warfare on the Atlantic with its storms and strong tides would be rather different from the kind of naval warfare Rome was used to in the Mediterranean. The Veneti fortified their hill forts, many of which were situated on isolated spits of land more accessible by sea than land, and centred their supplies in them. In addition they gathered together their allies from Aremorica (modern Brittany), the Channel coast, and even the British tribes with whom they traded.

Caesar divided his forces and sent them to campaign in different parts of northern and western Gaul, proof that his claims that Gaul was at peace or had been conquered were fundamentally untrue. Throughout his governorship, Caesar was worried about incursions by German tribes and always kept a strong force in the

Ardennes with cavalry to provide mobility against the Germans. This force also helped to hold down the Belgic tribes. Other forces were sent to Aquitania under Crassus and Normandy under Sabinus to impose Roman control more effectively than the cursory campaigns of the previous year. These legates did not have large forces at their disposal, and this perhaps reflects both Caesar's and Rome's expectations that small Roman forces should be able to defeat larger 'barbarian' forces without difficulty. Caesar himself led a force of nearly four legions to meet with his newly gathered fleet, probably near the mouth of the Loire.

The Veneti

The Venetic campaign was a tough one. Sieges and assaults took care of some of the hill forts but the wealth and resources of the Veneti were mobile and when one hill fort was about to be taken they loaded up their ships with people and possessions and simply sailed off to another. The newly built Roman fleet, designed for Mediterranean conditions and warfare, lacked the sturdiness needed to face Atlantic conditions and was stuck in harbour by the weather and sea conditions. The Romans, despite their professional army and sophisticated siege equipment, were facing an impasse and Caesar was forced to pause until his fleet could join him. Eventually the sea was calm enough to allow the Roman fleet to sail, and it encountered the Venetic navy off the coast of Brittany.

The size of the Roman fleet is not reported, but it consisted of Roman galleys, and ships provided by Rome's allies south of the Loire. The combined fleet of the Veneti and their allies numbered 220, although some may have been little more than fishing boats. The Venetic ships, designed for rough seas, were built of strong oak beams too sturdy to be rammed by the galleys and too high in the water for the effective use of missiles.

Under the command of Decimus Brutus (who was later one of Caesar's assassins), the Roman fleet prepared grappling hooks to take on the Gallic sailing ships and

then attacked. As with the famous *corvus*, the boarding bridge used against the mighty Carthaginian navy in the First Punic War, the Romans used the grappling hooks to overcome their disadvantage in naval warfare, cutting the rigging of the Gallic ships and rendering them helpless since they relied entirely on sail power. Unable to counter this new tactic, the Veneti decided to withdraw, at which point the wind dropped. Fortune favoured the Romans, who relied on oar power, and the galleys were able to go in and pick off the becalmed Venetic ships at their leisure. In an engagement lasting from late morning till sunset, most of the Venetic ships were destroyed.

Having lost their naval power in this decisive engagement, the Veneti could no longer retreat; they had nothing to protect them against the Romans or against other Gallic and British tribes and were forced to surrender. To serve as an example for detaining Roman officers and resisting Rome, Caesar executed the tribal leaders and sold the remainder of the population into slavery.

Normandy and Aquitania

Quintus Titurius Sabinus faced an increasingly powerful coalition of Gallic tribes including the Venelli, Curiosolites and Lexovii under the leadership of Viridovix, chief of the Unelli tribe. Unwilling to risk his smaller force in a pitched battle in the absence of Caesar, Sabinus resorted to a stratagem, keeping his troops in camp and refusing to sortie or deploy against the Gauls who were offering pitched battle, and so giving an impression of fear. This bolstered the Gauls' courage and they prepared to assault the Roman camp with brushwood to fill in the trenches. However, Sabinus had cleverly located his camp at the top of a long rise and by the time the charging Gauls reached the Roman defences their impetus was blunted and they were wearying. At this point Sabinus ordered his men to sortie and the fresh Romans were able to put the Gauls to flight with ease. All the tribes involved surrendered, placing the regions of modern Normandy under Roman control.

With just over one legion and a cavalry attachment, Publius Crassus had a tougher task against the tribes of Aquitania, so he raised additional infantry and cavalry from Provence and marched south of the Garonne and towards the Pyrenees, repulsing an attack by the Sontiates tribe on the marching column. There was

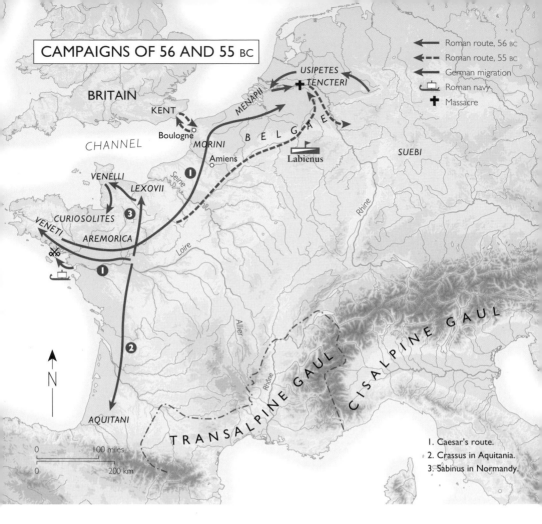

CAMPAIGNS OF 56 AND 55 BC

→ Roman route, 56 BC
→ Roman route, 55 BC
→ German migration
⬓ Roman navy
✝ Massacre

BRITAIN

KENT

CHANNEL

Boulogne

MORINI

Amiens

MENAPII

BELGAE

USIPETES
TENCTERI

SUEBI

Labienus

VENELLI

LEXOVII

CURIOSOLITES

VENETI

AREMORICA

Seine

Loire

Rhine

N

Allier

AQUITANI

Rhône

TRANSALPINE GAUL

CISALPINE GAUL

0   100 miles
0   200 km

1. Caesar's route.
2. Crassus in Aquitania.
3. Sabinus in Normandy.

more serious opposition from the Vocates and Tarusates who had Spanish allies who had fought alongside the rebel Roman general Sertorius in the 70s BC and brought with them their experience of fighting Roman armies. They aimed to cut Crassus off from his supply lines, a strategy that encouraged the Romans to seek pitched battle. But, drawing on the successful guerrilla tactics Sertorius had employed against Roman armies in Spain, the Gallic and Spanish tribes refused battle, instead blocking roads and supplies and attacking Crassus' marching column. If he wanted a result from the campaign, Crassus had to force an encounter, so his army attacked the enemy encampment. The camp was only properly fortified at the front, and once he learned of this, Crassus ordered reinforcements to circle round and attack the rear of the camp. The army of about 50,000 Gauls was taken by surprise and, completely surrounded, attempted to break out and flee, pursued by Crassus' cavalry force. Crassus reported to Caesar that only about 12,000 escaped the slaughter, and most of the tribes in the surrounding area surrendered. This was a significant victory and Crassus had succeeded in forcing the surrender of a huge area of south-western Gaul, including the Aquitani, who occupied land between the Pyrenees and the Garonne and who sent hostages to Crassus before they were demanded, thus avoiding a direct Roman attack on their lands.

Towards the end of summer, Caesar turned on the Morini and Menapii on the Channel coast. They had supported the Veneti and that was reason enough for an attack, but Caesar was probably already considering his campaigns for the following year, including a potential expedition across the Channel to Britain which would require a settled situation in northern Gaul. However, by this third year of Roman conquests in Gaul and the crushing victories inflicted by the Roman army in set-piece engagements like pitched battle and sieges, many Gallic tribes were changing their tactics and deliberately avoiding pitched battle, resorting instead to guerrilla warfare. The Morini and Menapii withdrew into their forested and marshy lands. Caesar probed these areas but came under attack when entrenching camp too close to the forest; whilst able to repulse the Gauls, the Romans were in danger of taking the pursuit too far into difficult terrain and losing the encounter, so Caesar withdrew. Because of the difficulties in engaging directly with the Gauls and heavy rainfall preventing further campaigning, Caesar resorted to ravaging farmland rather than engaging the enemy and he withdrew for the winter. The legions went into winter quarters in the land between the Loire and Saône that belonged to recently conquered tribes, their punishment for having resisted.

55 BC: Publicity stunts

Caesar's two campaigns of 55 BC were dictated as much by events in Rome as by military requirements in Gaul. This year his two closest political allies and at the same time his greatest rivals, Pompey and Crassus, were consuls in Rome. As chief magistrates of the Roman state, their positions enabled them to seize all the publicity, buy the people's affections and votes with gifts, grain, and public banquets, and wield considerable influence and patronage amongst their fellow senators. Aware of the need to remain in the public eye, Caesar decided to enhance his reputation by being the first Roman to lead an army across the Rhine into Germany and over the 'ocean' to the mysterious island of Britain. Caesar may well have been planning his expedition to Britain the previous year, the reason for pushing into the lands of the Morinii and Menapii so late into the campaigning season, but more urgent events on the continent meant that his extraordinary invasion of Britain took place probably later in the year than he had intended.

Two German tribes, the Usipetes and Tencteri, had crossed the Rhine in search of land after being ousted from their own by the stronger Suebi. Following the policy he had established with the migration of the Helvetii in his first year of office, Caesar refused to allow them to settle in Gaul but suggested that they settle in the territory of the Ubii who also had grievances with the Suebi, a solution that would have benefitted Caesar by strengthening pro-Roman opposition to the Suebi, but he also advanced aggressively towards the tribes who had their women and children with them. A short truce was established whilst the tribes consulted on the proposals, during which hostilities should have been suspended. Caesar claims that he ordered his cavalry out on patrol to abstain from fighting and that his cavalry force some 5,000 strong (actually made up largely of Gauls) was attacked by a German cavalry contingent. The 800 German cavalry managed to rout Caesar's cavalry despite the size differential, killing 74 but, significantly, breaking the truce. In retaliation, Caesar attacked their camp, caught them by surprise and massacred them, men, women and children, driving them into the nearby Rhine. Though there were probably nothing like the 430,000 casualties Caesar claims, it is likely that tens of thousands were killed, with no Roman losses. Roman warfare was often brutal, but this was excessively so. Caesar's enemies in Rome threatened to prosecute him for war crimes once his governorship and its accompanying immunity from prosecution came to an end.

Evidence of this slaughter has been identified by archaeological excavations near the town of Oss in the Netherlands at the confluence of the rivers Meuse and the Waal (the main branch of the Rhine). Skeletal remains have been identified from more than 70 individuals from the site of the river bed in antiquity (see page 104). Many show signs of battle trauma with bones damaged by blows from swords, spears and probably *pila*, including a number of skulls indicating fatal or near-fatal blows on the heads of those fleeing or inflicted when they were immobile on the ground. The skeletons were of warriors – swords, spearheads and other pieces of military equipment including the remains of helmets indicate this – and also of women, striking corroboration of the Caesarian narrative and the brutality of the war being waged by Caesar with high casualties inflicted on both fighters and non-combatants.

Caesar then decided to cross the Rhine to intimidate the Germans further, if they were not terrified enough by his massacre of the Usipetes and Tencteri. Because this was a publicity stunt to gain prestige among both the Germans and his fellow Romans, Caesar decided to build a bridge and march across the Rhine rather than simply row across or use pontoons: a bridge gave the impression of greater power and intent. The length

Silver *denarius* of Julius Caesar with a trophy made up of captured weapons, defeated Gaul and Gallia (the personification of Gaul). (Photo By DEA / A. RIZZI/De Agostini via Getty Images)

and detail in Caesar's description of the materials and construction of the bridge shows just how significant this move was, and how much of an impact he was expecting it to make in terms of both military verve and engineering prowess immediately to the German tribes and subsequently in reports to his audience, both hostile and supportive, in Rome. In ten days, his troops had built a timber bridge on wooden piles driven into the riverbed and Caesar marched into Germany, burned some empty villages, marched back before the powerful Suebic army could muster, and destroyed the bridge. The first Roman invasion of Germany lasted just 18 days.

The expedition to Britain was equally brief. Caesar crossed the Channel late in the campaigning season, his justification for the campaign being the military assistance the British tribes kept giving the Gauls, but that was a mere excuse. The expedition to Britain was hardly a full-scale invasion and was probably intended as an aggressive advance into the Britons' territory similar to that into Germany, and to impress Rome. Caesar took only two legions with him, the VII and X, and the cavalry force never got across the Channel, seriously limiting Roman operations. It is not known where in Kent Caesar landed: he had sent an officer, Gaius Volusenus, on a scouting mission and to identify possible landing places before the Romans embarked, but he only spent four days on this task and did so entirely from his ship. He appears to have failed to locate the large harbour at Richborough later used by Claudius, and when Caesar approached the coast near Dover he found the land-fall protected by cliffs and the Britons waiting. He moved seven miles up the coast to a flat, more open beach, probably at Walmer. The British had sent on their cavalry and chariots to oppose the landings and the deep-hulled Roman transports had to disembark the legionaries in deep water. Up to their waists in water and fully loaded with kit, the legionaries struggled ashore to be met by the terrifying 'barbarians', cavalry and chariots. Despite artillery support, the legionaries were reluctant to leave the safety of their ships. They were inspired to do so by the example set by the

OPPOSITE
Hellenistic sculpture of a wounded Gallic warrior, late 2nd century BC. (Photo by Universal History Archive/Universal Images Group via Getty Images)

famous eagle-bearer of the Tenth Legion. Jumping into the sea, this unnamed soldier forced his fellow legionaries to follow him by taking the standard into battle. To lose a standard was the ultimate disgrace and the soldiers of the Tenth Legion began disembarking. Once the scout ships began ferrying more legionaries to shore, the infantry was able to form up and force a landing. The Britons fled, but the failure of the cavalry to make the crossing meant the Romans were unable to finish the battle decisively. After a delayed embarkation from a different harbour further up the coast, the cavalry met strong tides and stormy weather and never managed to join the expeditionary force.

In the following days the Roman expeditionary force suffered nothing but setbacks. Apart from another failed attempt by the cavalry transports to cross, high tides caused serious damage to a number of the ships and transports on the beachhead that provided little protection for the vessels, and the small Roman force was in no position to winter in Britain, as it was inadequately supplied. To cap all this, a detachment of the VII Legion was ambushed while harvesting grain. Although a rescue party drove the British off, this only inspired them to gather a large force to attack the apparently vulnerable Romans. A short pitched battle ensued in front of the Roman encampment, but Caesar gives no details except that the Britons were easily repulsed and once again the lack of cavalry prevented any pursuit. Caesar demanded hostages from the defeated British tribes but could not wait for them to be handed over. With the rapidly approaching equinox and the likelihood of storms, Caesar withdrew having never got beyond the coast of Kent. The expedition to Britain could have been a disaster. Caesar had risked everything by leading an under-strength and poorly supplied force to Britain. But the crossing of the Channel caught the imagination of the Roman public more sharply even than the bridging of the Rhine. Caesar became a hero and a public thanksgiving of 20 days was decreed in Rome, very satisfactorily trumping the publicity and any popularity Pompey and Crassus had been able to achieve in the capital during their consulships.

54 BC: **Back to Britain**

A return to Britain the following year was inevitable. Despite the public thanks and plaudits, the expedition in 55 BC had been brief and achieved little; no booty had been acquired and, despite the promises, no hostages handed over. Roman prestige required a more robust action and preparations were made through the winter including the construction of transports suitable for operations in the Channel. Before embarking, Caesar took four lightly equipped legions and some cavalry on a swift operation against the Treveri to try to ensure their loyalty, at least temporarily, but it was clear that the situation was not properly secure in some parts of Gaul: Caesar took with him to Britain a number of Gallic leaders to ensure that they did not cause problems in his absence.

Leaving three legions and 2,000 cavalry to hold down northern Gaul, Caesar crossed to Britain with a force of five legions and a further 2,000 cavalry and landed unopposed on the coast of Kent. After disembarking, Caesar immediately took four of the legions and most of the cavalry to find the British who had gathered some 12 miles off. The Britons utilised hit-and-run tactics for most of the campaign and gained some success in hampering Caesar's advance. But the weather caused problems and again the ships were damaged by a storm. Caesar was compelled to return to the beachhead, fortify it securely and arrange for repairs to the ships before heading back out to find the British. The Britons used the delay to gather a larger army and unlike many of the Gallic tribes in their opposition to the Romans so far, the Britons were able to form an effective coalition under the leadership of Cassivellaunus, king of the powerful Catuvellauni tribe.

The mobility of the British infantry, cavalry and especially the chariots, caused the Romans problems and forced them to remain in close formation on the march lest they become isolated and picked off by the Britons. But when Cassivellaunus attacked a foraging party and was comprehensively repulsed, serious British

resistance was crushed. The Romans forced a crossing of the Thames at the only place fordable despite the Britons defending it, aiming for the Catuvellaunian capital, a hill fort surrounded by trees, perhaps Wheathampstead in Hertfordshire. At this point, various tribes began surrendering to Caesar, offering hostages and grain. Caesar's willingness to accept these overtures encouraged others to capitulate, and once the hill fort was easily taken by storm and a diversionary attack on the Roman bridgehead on the Kent coast repulsed, Cassivellaunus also requested terms. Eager to withdraw from Britain before the equinoctial storms, Caesar agreed, demanding hostages and an annual tribute paid to Rome. The second expedition to Britain was far more successful than the first and could truly be described as an invasion. Tribute had been exacted from the tribes and they could be considered subject to Rome – at least temporarily anyway: most of the tributes were short-lived although some formal contacts continued over the next century until the Claudian invasion. But Caesar had no need to return to the island, and events in Gaul prohibited that anyway.

The winter of 54/53 BC was one of considerable disturbance in Gaul, showing how superficial much of the Roman conquest had been. Poor harvests throughout the province caused by drought forced Caesar to divide his legions up when they went into winter quarters in north-eastern Gaul and probably increased discontent among the tribes who were forced to supply scarce grain to the occupying legions. The scattering of the legions provided an opportunity for the Gallic tribes, and within two weeks of being established, the winter camps were coming under co-ordinated attack.

Cotta and Sabinus

The furthest east of the winter camps, commanded by the legates Cotta and Sabinus, was the most exposed Roman base and therefore the one most vulnerable to attack. One legion (Caesar calls it inexperienced but it had in fact been campaigning for four years by this point) and five cohorts were attacked by the Eburones under their

dynamic leader Ambiorix, who claimed that all northern Gaul was in revolt and German mercenaries had crossed the Rhine to join in. He promised safe conduct to the Romans if they left their camp. Foolishly, Sabinus took him at his word and, despite the protestations of his fellow officers, he led his force out of the safety of camp in a formation inappropriate to the tactical situation, straight into an ambush the Gauls had laid in a steep-sided valley. The Roman marching column panicked, unable to maintain proper formation in terrain that denied them any opportunity to manoeuvre. The Romans were wiped out, Sabinus ignominiously being killed when trying to parley with Ambiorix, whom he still felt he could trust. A few escaped with their lives; others made it back to the encampment where they committed suicide during the night to avoid capture.

OPPOSITE
Statue of Ambiorix in Tongres. Set up in 1866, the statue represents freedom and resistance to invaders. (Photo by: Arterra/Universal Images Group via Getty Images)

News of the second campaign in Britain

We are waiting for the outcome of the war in Britain. It's known that the approaches to the island are surrounded by wall-like cliffs. It's also been established that there isn't a scrap of silver in the island and no hope of booty except for slaves – and I don't suppose you're expecting them to know much about literature or music!

- Marcus Cicero, letter to Atticus, *c.* 1 July 54 BC.

On 24 October I received letters from my brother Quintus and from Caesar, sent from the nearest point on the coast of Britain on 25 September. The campaign in Britain is over, hostages have been taken, there's no booty, but tribute has been paid and they are bringing back the army from Britain.

- Marcus Cicero, letter to Atticus, late October 54 BC.

Quintus Cicero

Quintus Cicero, the brother of Rome's most famous orator, had one legion encamped in the territory of the Nervii. Encouraged by the massacre of Sabinus' force, the Aduatuci, Nervii and their dependent tribes attacked Cicero's camp, trying to sell him the same story

Trajan's Column (early 2nd century AD). A Roman encampment comes under attack. (akg-images)

about general revolt and a German invasion. Unlike Sabinus, Cicero refused point blank to discuss terms, strengthened the camp's defences and tried frantically to contact Caesar. Under guidance from Roman prisoners, the Nervii built a circumvallation of rampart and ditch and moved siege towers up to the Roman fortifications. There followed a desperate couple of weeks in which the legion successfully held off attacks that continued both day and night. Cicero's troops refused to leave the ramparts even when the barracks were fired and their possessions were burning, but injuries were taking their toll. By the time Caesar relieved the siege, the legion had suffered 90 per cent casualties.

When Cicero did finally get a message to Caesar, he acted immediately, redeploying his legions and hurrying by forced marches to Nervian territory, covering up to 20 miles a day. Though he had only two legions and a small cavalry force, Caesar destroyed a 60,000-strong Nervian army which had abandoned its siege of Cicero's camp to head off the relieving army. Cicero's dogged resistance and the outstanding bravery of his officers won high praise from Caesar. His narrative of these events includes the tale of the two centurions Pullo and Vorenus who competed with each other in bravery as they fought the Gauls, each saving the other's life during the desperate engagements as they sought to prove themselves worthy of promotion to the position of senior centurion in the legion.

53 BC: Operations in the north

Following the disastrous winter of 54 BC, the season's campaigns concentrated on re-establishing Roman superiority in north-eastern Gaul. Caesar recruited two more legions and borrowed one from Pompey, bringing the total to ten (40,000–50,000 legionaries). The size of the army allowed operations to be conducted, often simultaneously, against numerous tribes who had either been involved in the winter's uprisings or whom Caesar did not trust. At the end of the campaign most of the legions were quartered together on the Senones; the remaining four were quartered in pairs on the Treveri and Lingones, to prevent a repeat of the previous winter's attacks.

Before the campaigning season had properly begun, Caesar launched a surprise attack, concentrating on destroying property and capturing prisoners and cattle. The Nervii were swiftly forced to surrender and the legions returned to winter quarters.

A 1st-century AD terracotta relief of a Roman soldier guarding a Gallic prisoner, with captured weapons hung from a tree as a trophy. (Lanmas / Alamy Stock Photo)

In early spring Caesar marched suddenly on the Senones, taking them before they were able to withdraw into their *oppidum*. With their people and supplies vulnerable, they had no alternative but to surrender.

Caesar then marched into the Rhine delta with seven legions. Menapian tactics were to withdraw into the marshes, but the Romans built causeways to allow them access to the area, then destroyed all their property, capturing cattle and taking prisoners as they advanced. With their wealth destroyed, the Menapii were forced to surrender.

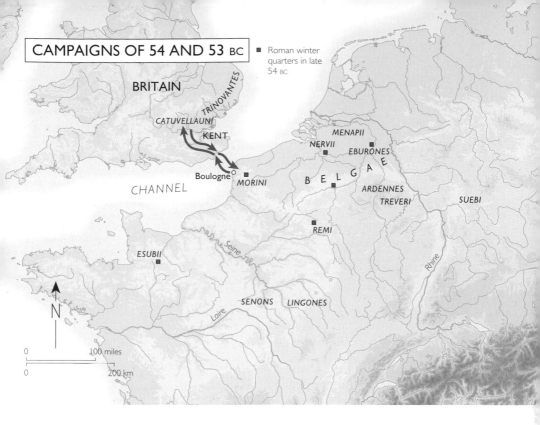

BRITAIN

TRINOVANTES

CATUVELLAUNI

KENT

CHANNEL

Boulogne

MORINI

MENAPII

NERVII

EBURONES

B E L G A E

ARDENNES

TREVERI

SUEBI

REMI

Rhine

ESUBII

Seine

SENONS   LINGONES

Loire

N

0 ───── 100 miles
0 ───── 200 km

The Treveri were still unsettled after the winter and were awaiting promised German reinforcements before attacking Labienus, who was encamped with 25 cohorts of legionaries and a large cavalry force. Keen to defeat the Treveri before help arrived, Labienus lured them into attacking on terrain that was very unfavourable to them. Labienus pretended to be withdrawing and the Treveri charged up a very steep riverbank to fall on the Romans. The Romans formed up their battle line and the Treveri, disordered and out of breath from their uphill charge, were routed within minutes of the battle commencing; Labienus' powerful cavalry force mopped up those fleeing. Help would never be forthcoming from the Germans now, so the whole tribe of Treveri surrendered.

For a second time Caesar bridged the Rhine and marched into Germany to punish the tribes for sending help to the Gauls and discourage them from doing so again. He used the same bridge design as in 55 BC, very close to the location of his first crossing. Supply problems

limited the scope of operations and Caesar seems to have been unwilling to risk battle against the powerful Suebi so he withdrew, but he had shown that he could cross the Rhine and attack German lands at will.

In the Ardennes two columns of three legions each raided much of modern Belgium, destroying property and taking prisoners. The burning of crops threatened the Gauls with starvation and many tribes, including the Eburones, surrendered.

In the space of a year, northern Gaul was totally reduced through vicious punitive raids aimed at destroying the property and wealth of the tribes.

52 BC: **The great revolt**

In the winter of 53/52 BC the general revolt which had been threatening erupted, perhaps because the tribes realised that co-ordinated resistance could prove effective against the Romans, and possibly because a tribal council Caesar held the previous year suggested that Gaul was now to be treated as a province of Rome. Taking advantage of Caesar's return to northern Gaul and the political turmoil and uncertainties in Rome caused by the death of the popular politician Publius Clodius, the Gauls began to plan their campaign. Amongst the tribes leading the call for revolt was the Carnutes, whose territory included consecrated land supposed to be the centre of Gaul, and where the druids met annually to settle disputes between Gauls. This sacred space was now being threatened by Roman advances and was of interest to all Gauls, encouraging them to put aside their previous differences. Significantly, the Gauls found a charismatic leader to bring the tribes together and lead a united resistance to Rome. A young and popular chieftain of the Arvernian tribe, Vercingetorix became the focal point of resistance, and this year of campaigning is presented by Caesar as the crux of his conquest of Gaul.

The revolt began in Cenabum (Orleans), the tribal capital of the Carnutes. In an organised attack, all the Roman citizens in the town were massacred; most were merchants but the victims included a Roman of equestrian rank whom Caesar had put in charge of the grain supply. The action was designed to ignite rebellion, but may also have been done in the expectation that Caesar would respond swiftly, perhaps without sufficient preparation early in the campaigning season, and run into difficulties with support and logistics. Caesar, who had been in Italy, reacted in his usual way when the Gauls committed violence against Roman citizens and particularly against his officers. He moved extremely swiftly to enact retribution and to try to prevent the whole of Gaul going up in revolt and rushed to Provence with a small force. Having arranged the defence of Roman territory, Caesar marched through the Massif Central and used Agedincum (Sens) as his base. His first task was to avenge the Roman massacre at Cenabum and this was done with no delay, a night attack on the town to prevent the inhabitants, the Bituriges, from fleeing. Virtually the whole population was captured and Caesar handed them on to his soldiers as spoils after sacking and destroying the town. Caesar then moved to threaten Arvernian territory, forcing Vercingetorix to abandon an attack on Gorgobina, capital of the Boii, who remained staunchly allied to Caesar.

The Roman route detoured in order to capture several *oppida* (the towns of Vellaunodunum, Cenabum, and Noviodunum), partly to spread terror, but perhaps more importantly, to capture supplies of grain and fodder. As it was still winter there was no forage available and the Roman army was finding it difficult to supply itself. The Gauls realised this and Vercingetorix's strategy was to avoid general engagements with the Romans, instead attacking foraging parties and supply trains. The Gauls cut off the Romans from all sources of food by withdrawing the population and supplies to the strongest *oppida* and adopting a scorched-earth policy, abandoning all other *oppida*. Vercingetorix did not want to defend the *oppidum* of Avaricum (Bourges) despite its strong defences, but was persuaded to do so by the Bituriges who occupied it. Caesar immediately invested it.

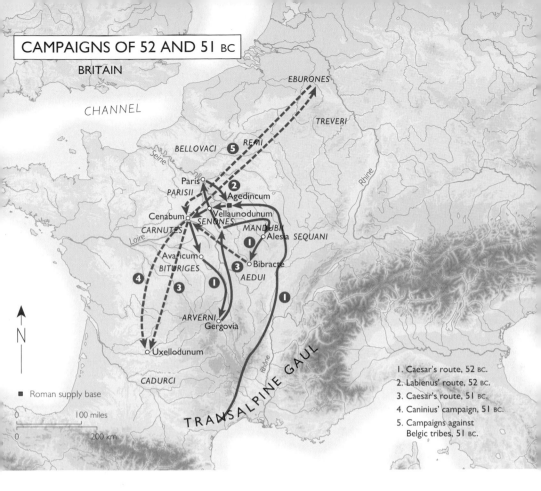

BRITAIN

CHANNEL

EBURONES

TREVERI

BELLOVACI ⑤ REMI

Paris ②
PARISII Agedincum

Cenabum Vellaunodunum
CARNUTES SENONES MANDUBII
  Alesia SEQUANI
  ①

Avaricum ③ ① Bibracte
BITURIGES AEDUI

④ ③ ①

ARVERNI ①
Gergovia

Uxellodunum

CADURCI

TRANSALPINE GAUL

N

0 ____ 100 miles
0 ____ 200 km

Roman supply base

1. Caesar's route, 52 BC.
2. Labienus' route, 52 BC.
3. Caesar's route, 51 BC.
4. Caninius' campaign, 51 BC.
5. Campaigns against Belgic tribes, 51 BC.

The swift abandonment of the Gallic strategy may suggest that Vercingetorix's leadership of a united Gallic coalition was not entirely solid, and Caesar may have exaggerated the dangers of the campaigns of the year for political and literary effect, but nonetheless the situation for the Romans was dangerous.

Avaricum

The *oppidum* had strong fortifications and was virtually surrounded by a river and marshes, but Caesar entrenched where there was a gap in the natural defences and constructed a siege terrace of earth and timber 330 feet wide and 80 feet high. Despite the cold, rain, sorties and attempts by the Gauls to undermine and fire the terrace, probably drawing on their experiences from mining, the Roman siege works were completed in only 25 days. Camped with a large force outside the *oppidum*, Vercingetorix had unsuccessfully tried to attack Roman foraging parties and wanted to abandon the defence of Avaricum before it was captured. He was unable to persuade those whose home it was to do so, however: they were confident in the strength of their defences. Under cover of a heavy rainstorm when the Gallic sentries were less vigilant, Caesar ordered siege towers into position and his troops to assault the walls. The Gauls valiantly but vainly defended the breach and the Roman artillery took its toll, clearing an entrance for the legionaries who then took possession of the circuit of walls without risking street fighting by descending into the town proper. Once possession of the fortifications was secured the soldiers turned from disciplined attack to rape and pillage. No prisoners were taken and Caesar claims 40,000 died. This, he notes, was the punishment for the massacre at Cenabum in the winter.

Vercingetorix

An ambitious young noble of the Arvernian tribe whose father had been executed for attempting to make himself king, Vercingetorix was ejected from the tribe by his uncle and other tribal leaders. They opposed his attempt to raise rebellion, but he was nonetheless able to raise a force and take control of the Arverni, then succeed where no other Gallic leader had, by forging an army under single leadership to resist Rome. Although he ultimately failed in his attempt to rid Gaul of the Romans, Vercingetorix was promoted in later French culture as representative of freedom, resistance and nationalism. Napoleon III had a monument and a seven-metre-tall statue of Vercingetorix erected at Alesia, the site of his last stand, in 1865.

Gold *stater* of Vercingetorix, the Arvernian chieftain who united Gaul in resistance to the Romans. (Photo by Eric BRISSAUD/Gamma-Rapho via Getty Images)

Artillery

Catapults were an important weapon in the armoury of the Roman army and were the ancient equivalent of artillery and machine guns. Torsion artillery had been invented by the Greeks in the 4th century BC and developed during the subsequent Hellenistic period. By the late 1st century BC the machines available were both sophisticated and highly effective in warfare. There were two basic types of catapults, the *ballista*, which hurled stones, and the *scorpion*, which fired missiles similar to the later crossbow. The catapults were powered by coils of rope or sinew, which could be tightened up using a ratchet, and when the stored energy was released, the missile could be projected with terrific speed and noise. Specialist architects and engineers who would build and maintain these machines were attached to Roman armies, but in the field they would have been operated by the soldiers. In addition to the greater firepower such catapults provided

Modern reconstruction of a *scorpion*, a Roman bolt-shooting catapult. These powerful and accurate artillery machines significantly increased the Roman army's firepower. (© M.C. Bishop)

to Roman armies, the presence of these engines of war on the battlefield or before a besieged town must have put considerable psychological pressure on the enemy. Gallic armies and communities were unused to such complex machinery; having to face a *scorpion* on the battlefield with its vicious sting cannot have been something they would have relished, and the very prospect of these machines may have put the Gauls at a disadvantage. Artillery mounted in boats was used, along with slingers and archers, to provide covering fire for the landings in Britain in 54 BC; Caesar says that the Britons were unnerved by the machines as they had never seen anything like them before, and this helped to drive them off the beaches.

Despite their technological superiority though, not all catapults were appropriate to Gallic warfare. Both types of catapults used by Roman armies were essentially anti-personnel devices. Although the largest stone-throwing *ballistae* might have been able to cause some damage to stone fortifications, they were not used primarily to knock down walls from afar: that was the job of battering rams and mines. They would have had far less impact, in any case, against the earth ramparts of *oppida*, the *murus Gallicus*, a combination of earth, timber and stone ramparts that fortified some *oppida*. Additionally, they were large and not particularly mobile, and given the speed with which Caesar frequently operated and the straightforward nature of most of the siege warfare he encountered, these larger catapults were probably not used. The *scorpions*, however, were much more mobile and could be used in both open warfare and sieges, adding to the missile barrage fired upon an enemy army in the opening phases of a pitched battle, for example. In preparation for a possible pitched battle against the Belgae, Caesar had ordered the construction of trenches to protect his battle line and prevent outflanking manoeuvres by the enemy. At the end of each trench a redoubt was dug and artillery positioned in them. Had battle ensued, the *scorpions* in the redoubts would have provided considerable protection to the Roman army's flanks. Years later in the 'mopping-up' operations of 51 BC, Caesar positioned his battle line so that if pitched battle

occurred against the Bellovaci, their battle line would be well within reach of the Roman artillery. While a volley of *pila* might be visible and Gallic warriors knew what to expect, *scorpion* bolts were swift, silent and deadly. To be killed by one would not have been as glorious as being killed by an enemy warrior or soldier in open battle. In neither case, however, did the Gauls accept pitched battle: Caesar had so weighted the odds in his favour through use of topography and siting of artillery that the Gauls refused to engage. They were undoubtedly brave warriors, but they were not so stupid as to throw their lives away.

Most Roman camps would have been defended by artillery and it is surprising that Caesar does not mention it having any role in defending Quintus Cicero's winter camp, which came under a sustained Gallic assault in the winter of 54 BC. It is unlikely that Cicero's winter quarters

Trajan's Column, early 2nd century AD. Roman legionaries build artillery emplacements from felled trees. (akg-images)

would not have been equipped with *scorpions* positioned in the gates and towers of the fortifications, something that was required by 2nd-century AD Roman textbooks on fortifying camps. Such artillery would have been especially useful as the legionary strength defending the camp was depleted by the deaths and injuries that Caesar reports. It seems to have been the artillery that made the difference a few years later when an under-manned Roman camp at Gergovia came under attack by the Gauls: the machines could fire several bolts a minute and required far less physical effort to operate than hurling *pila* or lunging at the enemy with spears. When used by skilled operators, moreover, the *scorpions* could be deadly accurate.

The accuracy of *scorpions* is best illustrated through their role in Roman siege warfare. Carefully sited artillery could keep the defenders off the walls, while other soldiers operated battering rams, scaled with ladders or conducted undermining operations at the bottom of ramparts. At Avaricum they provided some protection for the legionaries constructing the huge siege terrace, at least until the besieged Gauls sortied *en masse*. But they were initially ineffective in preventing the Gauls from trying to set fire to the terrace. The Gaul who was throwing incendiary material onto the terrace was killed by a *scorpion*, but then another took his place. Caesar says they continued sacrificing themselves in attempting to fire the terrace and the *scorpion* kept on killing them until the fire went out and they gave up the effort. A *scorpion* must have been trained on one point and was able to fire accurate missiles one after the other. Accurate artillery also helped to end the last siege of the conquest, at Uxellodunum in 51 BC. *Scorpions* positioned in towers prevented the Gauls from getting access to their only remaining water supply, though they did not actually surrender until the spring feeding the supply was diverted.

The Gallic coalition

Despite the setback at Avaricum, Vercingetorix had the authority to maintain the Gallic coalition and it was strengthened by the revolt of the Aedui, long-standing allies of Caesar. Some Aedui remained loyal and Caesar continued to command and use Aeduan cavalry, but it caused another blow to his already precarious supply lines, although the capture of supplies at Avaricum must have helped. Now the campaigning season had begun and fodder was becoming available in the open, Caesar ordered Labienus with four legions and cavalry to crush the Parisii and Senones, while he marched the remaining six legions down the river Allier to Gergovia. Unlike Avaricum, which Vercingetorix had not wished to defend, this was one of the *oppida* he did intend to hold, probably because it was very strongly fortified, but perhaps also because it was the hill fort of his own tribe, the Arverni.

Gergovia

The hilly terrain dominated the Gergovia campaign. On arrival the Romans as usual entrenched camp, then captured a high hill opposite the *oppidum*, which dominated the principal water supply. Caesar had a smaller camp constructed there and linked his two camps with a wide ditch. This allowed him to move his forces around without interference from enemy sorties or cavalry. The next step was to capture another hill much closer to the hill fort and which actually adjoined the *oppidum*. The Gauls were not patrolling it properly and the legionaries were able to take it without much difficulty, crossing a six foot wall built to prevent such an action. These initial Roman actions look very much like the strategy that had been employed at Avaricum, establishing positions before exploring weaknesses in the fortifications and building siege works and towers for an assault.

Indeed, in his *Commentaries* Julius Caesar claims he was only intending to take this hill and then halt the action. Either the soldiers failed to hear the recall he claimed to have sounded and disobeyed orders, or he had actually intended to launch an attack against the *oppidum* itself if this first phase proved successful. Whatever the truth, the Romans did proceed to make a concerted direct attack on Gergovia's defences, the enthusiasm of the centurions for being the first onto the walls and displaying their courage

Stone wall of the Gallic *oppidum* of Gergovia, the well-defended capital of the Arverni. (Romary, Wikimedia Commons, CC BY-SA 3.0)

in the competition for awards and promotion driving them on against the defenders who hugely outnumbered them. The Romans were driven back but were saved from rout by the presence of other legionaries formed up outside Gergovia which discouraged Vercingetorix from pursuing. In total 700 Romans were killed including 46 centurions, an extraordinarily high casualty rate amongst these key officers who had driven forward the rash attack but then fought with notable bravery and sacrificed their lives to allow their men to escape. Caesar blamed his centurions and soldiers for the defeat and may have been less than clear in reporting his intentions in his *Commentaries* to distance himself from blame for a serious setback. He offered pitched battle in an attempt to restore a bit of Roman prestige but not surprisingly Vercingetorix refused: he had

just scored a significant victory over the Romans and in any case the Gallic strategy was specifically to avoid such set-piece engagements where the Romans had the advantage. Instead a minor cavalry skirmish ensued which allowed Caesar to note a Roman success before his withdrawal.

Caesar's forced withdrawal from Gergovia must have greatly increased Vercingetorix's reputation and encouraged more tribes to join the revolt. He continued to attack the Roman supply lines while calling in reinforcements. The Romans, too, obtained reinforcements, from the Germans who proved effective in routing the Gallic cavalry attacks on the Roman marching columns. The next *oppidum* Vercingetorix decided to defend was Alesia in the territory of the Mandubii and after the victory at Gergovia he must have been confident of success.

Labienus meanwhile was dealing with the Parisii and Senones and Caesar recounts his campaign in detail, partly because of his legate's brilliant tactics which led to a notable success after the difficulties at Gergovia. With his four legions Labienus began investing Lutetia (Paris) and engaging the Senones, but on learning of events at Gergovia, the revolt of the Aedui, and a rising amongst the nearby Bellovaci which threatened his positions, he decided to withdraw and rejoin Caesar. After defeating the Parisii and Senones in pitched battle, through clever manoeuvring Labienus deceived the Gauls into thinking there were two Roman armies operating in the area, leading to them dividing their forces. Labienus was able to surround one depleted Gallic army and destroy it, defeat the remainder with his cavalry and withdraw safely to rejoin Caesar.

Alesia

Located about 30 miles north-west of modern Dijon, Alesia was a large hill fort on a lozenge-shaped plateau protected by steep slopes and rivers on two sides. There was a plain at one end and at the other, the eastern end, Vercingetorix's united Gallic army was encamped. It was clear that an assault was out of the question, particularly after Gergovia, as Caesar could not risk another reverse, so the Romans would have to blockade. This was Vercingetorix's intention, for he allowed himself to be hemmed in at Alesia and ordered a relieving army to be gathered with all possible speed. The intention was to catch the static Roman army in a pincer movement with simultaneous attacks by the besieged under Vercingetorix and a relieving army, which Caesar claims (perhaps dubiously) consisted of nearly a quarter of a million infantry and 8,000 cavalry. Caesar describes the siege of Alesia in detail: the size and complexity of the siege works would have impressed both the Gauls and Roman audiences and the siege is presented as the decisive engagement in the crushing of the Gallic revolt, with Caesar's own arrival at a crucial point in a pressing attack on Roman positions the decisive moment.

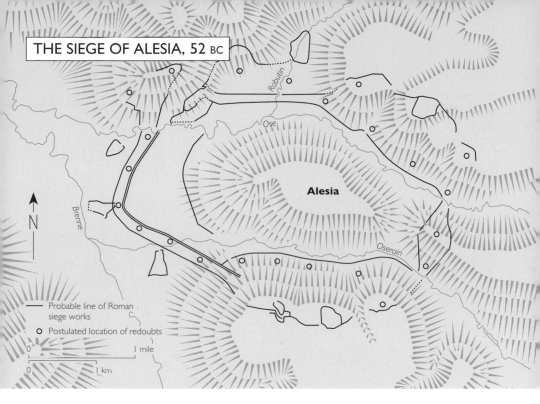

Alesia

Rabutin

Ose

Brenne

Oserain

N

—— Probable line of Roman siege works

O Postulated location of redoubts

0   1 mile

0   1 km

The Roman siege works at Alesia were extraordinary in their size and complexity. After digging a deep ditch on the plain to prevent cavalry attacks on the working parties, the Romans built a rampart with palisade and towers at regular intervals fronted by a double ditch, one filled with water diverted from the rivers where possible; seven camps and 23 redoubts were added at strategic points. This line covered a circuit of 11 miles. Caesar was not happy even with this formidable system of defences, and lines of booby traps were extended for several yards in front of the trenches. These comprised rows of sharpened stakes (*cippi* or grave-markers), then covered pits with sharpened stakes planted in them (*lilia* or lillies), and finally rows of wooden stakes with barbed iron spikes stuck into them (*stimuli* or spurs). Once this circuit was completed Caesar had another identical line built outside, this one 14 miles in circumference, to protect the besiegers from the relieving army. The whole system took about a month to construct and must have had a profound impact on the environment given the amount of timber required and

Reconstruction of the Roman siege works at Alesia, MuséoParc Alésia. These formidable defences protected Caesar's army from attacks from both the besieged and the massive relieving army raised by Vercingetorix. (Patrick, Flickr, CC BY-SA 2.0)

foraging by Caesar's legions. Archaeological investigations have indicated that the fortifications were not as complete as Caesar suggests. There may have been gaps in the lines, particularly where the terrain provided natural protection, but the systems held up to concerted attacks by both Gallic armies even when they were prepared with bridging materials to cross the outer defences and ditches.

Vercingetorix meanwhile dismissed his cavalry since there would be little use for them in a siege and more importantly the horses would eat valuable supplies. He attempted to extend his limited supplies by sending away the non-combatants, and to disrupt – unsuccessfully – the Roman siege works by sorties whilst waiting for the Gallic relief army to arrive.

Ultimately, however, the Romans did not have to starve out the defenders at Alesia, and no attempts were made to take the *oppidum* by assault. Violent co-ordinated attacks by both Gallic forces on the Roman siege works had no effect and although the lines came under enormous pressure in one attack, Roman reinforcements arrived in time as did Caesar, clearly visible to his men because of the distinctive colour of his general's cloak, and this turned the tide of the engagement; the Gauls were repulsed. It became clear that the extraordinary defences the Roman army had constructed were not going to break and both the failure of the revolt and starvation for those shut up in Alesia were inevitable. Vercingetorix surrendered and the relieving army disbanded. Large numbers of prisoners were taken and Caesar distributed most of them amongst his men in lieu of booty. He spared the Arverni and his former allies the Aedui, though required them to provide large numbers of hostages to ensure compliance. Vercingetorix was kept prisoner in Italy, to be displayed six years later in Caesar's triumphal procession in Rome, after which he was ritually strangled.

The surrender of Vercingetorix

The leader Vercingetorix put on his finest armour and equipped his horse magnificently, then sallied out of the gate. After riding several times around Caesar who was sitting on a dais, he then dismounted, took off his armour and set himself at Caesar's feet where he remained in silence until Caesar ordered the guard to take him away and keep him for his triumph.
- Plutarch, *Life of Julius Caesar*

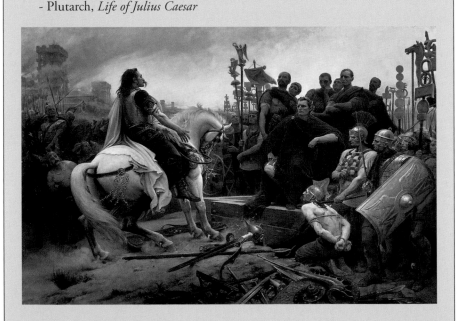

Vercingetorix throws down his arms at the feet of Julius Caesar, French artist Lionel Royer's 1899 representation of the Gallic chieftain's surrender. (Photo by Fine Art Images/Heritage Images/Getty Images)

51–50 BC: Mopping up

The legions were distributed throughout Gaul over the winter to keep down the defeated tribes and to protect the Remi who alone had been unswerving in their support for Rome. Caesar's last full year of campaigning in Gaul involved mid-winter terror raids against the Bituriges and Carnutes and, once spring had begun, Roman forces were sent which brutally crushed all remaining thought of rebellion amongst the Belgic tribes, the Bellovaci, Eburones, Treveri and Carnutes. The only remaining serious resistance was in south-western Gaul. Here two men, Drappes, a Senonian who was nonetheless able to exert influence among other tribes, and Lucterius, a local Cadurcan, took over the *oppidum* of Uxellodunum which was extremely well fortified.

Commius

One of the Gallic rebellion's leaders was Commius, chieftain of the Gallic Atrebates and an early ally of Caesar. He travelled to Britain in advance of the 55 BC expedition to gather intelligence for the Romans, and the following year negotiated the surrender of the British king Cassivellaunus. His reward was control over the neighbouring Morini and exemption from taxation for the Atrebates, but Commius fell out with the Romans and joined Vercingetorix's rebellion. Commius was one of the commanders of the relieving army at Alesia and in 51 BC he stirred up further rebellion amongst the Bellovaci. Labienus tried to have him assassinated at a parley but Commius escaped and later fled to Britain where he was able to establish himself as king of the British Atrebates.

Uxellodunum

With only two legions, the Roman legate Caninius invested the *oppidum*, building three camps at strategic points and starting a circumvallation. Drappes and Lucterius clearly knew what to expect because they sortied to collect supplies, but were intercepted by Caninius, and Drappes was captured. Roman reinforcements arrived during the siege, and Caesar personally attended for the final crushing of the revolt.

The 'rules of war'

When the Gallic *oppidum* of the Aduatuci was being besieged by the Romans, the tribal leaders sent envoys requesting peace. Caesar replied that he would be merciful and spare the tribe, 'provided that they surrendered before the battering ram touched the wall of the *oppidum*'.

There were no rules laid down in antiquity about the treatment of the defeated in war. Ancient custom gave the victor total and absolute power over the defeated, whether they had surrendered voluntarily or been forced into submission. Defeated peoples, both combatants and non-combatants, could be executed, sold into slavery or even released, and their treatment was totally dependent on the decision of the victorious commander. Important captives, those of high social or political status, might be treated better than ordinary people, or they might be executed to set an example to others. Setting an example was one of the main factors in deciding the fate of the defeated, and linked with this were the overall aims of the conqueror. The difficulty of the campaign or battle might also have affected how the victor treated the conquered, along with whether the losing side

had committed any atrocities during the course of the war. The slaughter of civilians at Avaricum was so brutal, Caesar tells us, because the siege had been a hard one and the Roman soldiers were avenging the massacre of Roman civilians at Cenabum.

We hear little of the Gallic treatment of Roman prisoners. Caesar gives a graphic description of the immolation of captured warriors by Gauls as a sacrifice to the Gallic war god Esus, but does not report this happening to any Roman captives.

This 1st-century AD relief from Paris shows the Gallic god Esus who continued to be worshipped after the Roman conquest. (Photo by CM Dixon/Print Collector/Getty Images)

Despite the disaster that befell Drappes' foraging party, Uxellodunum was very well supplied and the forces bottled up there were nothing like as numerous as those at Alesia the previous year. Potentially they could have held out for some time, but Caesar was keen to take the town swiftly to serve as an example and so attacked the water supply. Like many Gallic *oppida*, Uxellodunum was dependent on an external water supply, and artillery was set up to cut the defenders off from the rivers, leaving only a spring from which water could be obtained. The Romans then built a huge ramp and tower to dominate the spring and fire on those collecting water and secretly dug tunnels towards it. Parts of the tunnels were discovered by archaeologists in the 19th century. The Gauls sortied in an attempt to destroy the siege ramp, rolling flaming casks down onto the woodwork, but their diversionary attack was repulsed and the Roman soldiers were able to extinguish the incendiary devices before serious damage was done. Finally, the Roman tunnels reached the spring and the Gauls, ignorant of what had caused their ever-reliable spring to run dry, interpreted it as a divine signal and surrendered. Instead of massacring the defenders, Caesar cut off their hands and set them free to serve as an example of the punishment meted out to those who resisted Rome.

So Gaul was conquered, or at least the tribes had all surrendered to Roman power. The legions were brigaded throughout Gaul over the winter and virtually no campaigning took place the following year because all significant resistance had been crushed, and Caesar had already turned his attention back to Rome. Civil war was becoming inevitable and Caesar would be one of the key players.

THE WORLD AROUND WAR
The impact of the conflict

War was central to the lives of both Romans and Gauls. In both societies one of the most effective ways for the aristocracy to maintain status was to be successful in war, and warfare touched upon the lives of everyone, rich and poor. For the Gauls, though, the Gallic War was different from the kinds of conflict they usually experienced in its range, intensity and destructiveness. Wars in Gaul tended to be on a fairly small scale, often little more than raiding parties against neighbours to grab easily portable property, livestock and slaves. These allowed the elite warriors to maintain their positions of authority in their tribes by demonstrating prowess in battle and the acquisition of wealth, which benefited the whole tribe. In particular the aristocratic leaders were able to display their position through the purchase of other 'status' goods from abroad, mostly from the Greek and Roman cities of southern Gaul. Younger warriors, too, could make their names through these raids and begin to acquire wealth. On a wider level, successful raiding increased a tribe's military reputation and could lead to the subjection of neighbouring tribes to dependent status, thereby lessening the likelihood of attack by other tribes. After the defeat of the Helvetii, for example, the Aedui allowed the beaten Boii to settle on their

land because of their reputation for valour: the Boii would have become dependent on the Aedui, thus increasing the latter's military strength and influence in inter-tribal relations. So pressing was the need for increasing prestige in this way, that the Arverni and Sequani enlisted the help of German warriors in their campaign against the Aedui. Such raids caused some destruction and loss of property, including cattle, and Gallic peasants were often captured to be sold into slavery, but permanent conquests were rare.

The Roman approach to warfare was different. Whilst the Celtic style of warfare involved mainly those of warrior status with those of lower status involved when necessary, Roman society not only expected regular wars of conquest, but was prepared for it. A governor in Caesar's position would have been expected to campaign and possibly conquer new territory, and he had access to forces drawn from a mixture of conscripts and volunteers. The extra legions that were raised for the war in Gaul (six further legions during Caesar's governorship) were unlikely to have put considerable strain on the manpower of Italy. The majority of recruits came from northern Italy and many would probably have welcomed the opportunity to serve in the legions (especially as many of them may well not have possessed full Roman citizenship and legionary service would have allowed them to assert their claims to it). Military service meant full integration into the Roman state, and the opportunity for enrichment from booty. So in terms of manpower and resources, the conquest of Gaul had little impact on the Roman state: it was, quite simply, what Rome expected. For the Gauls though, the intensity of Roman campaigning and particularly the speed with which their lands were reduced to provincial status must have been a terrible shock.

One of the main reasons for the extraordinary speed of the Roman conquest was the failure, or inability, of the Gauls to co-operate in their own defence, in contrast to the Celtic tribes in Britain. Caesar took

advantage of the rivalry between Gallic tribes and when they were eventually combined under the leadership of Vercingetorix in 52 BC, it was too late to prevent the permanent establishment of Rome in Gaul and the creation of Roman provinces. We hear little from Caesar about the effects of the war on Gaul and its population (his audience would not have been particularly interested in these kinds of detail), but the effects must have been widespread, affecting the lives of wealthy and poor, influential and unimportant alike. Despite the turmoil caused by the campaigns of conquest though, the establishment of the Roman provinces ensured the continuation of the Gallic aristocracy in their dominance over the lower orders.

Loss of life

The biographer Plutarch claims that Caesar captured more than 800 towns, subdued 300 tribes, slew a million Gauls in the fighting and captured more. Whilst these figures are no doubt heavily over-exaggerated, they nonetheless give us an idea of the huge scale of the campaigns and Gallic losses. Men, women and children were legitimate targets in ancient warfare. Those tilling the soil or tending animals might be captured and carried off as slaves, or slaughtered by Romans in search of supplies or casual plunder. Such actions might be sanctioned by Roman officers and might even be organised on a large scale, particularly in the search for supplies, or carried out on the initiative of soldiers without their superiors' knowledge since there was unlikely to be serious punishment for such minor misdemeanours. The civilian population was particularly at risk because of the speed with which the Roman army moved: they could easily be caught out in the open, too far from the supposed shelter provided by *oppida*. During the campaigns of early 52 BC, Caesar's men regularly caught civilians in their fields and villages, as did the Gauls, who posed just as serious a risk to civilians from tribes who still supported Rome. Very high civilian casualties must have been caused during the destruction of the Helvetian army at the very beginning of the conquest, since the Helvetian warriors' families were at the battle site, watching from their wagons. They were almost certainly caught up in the slaughter following the capture by Roman soldiers of the Helvetian encampment. Worse was the massacre of the Usipetes and Tencteri. The Roman troops fell on a poorly fortified encampment and met only minor resistance.

Caesar noted, 'Because they had brought all their possessions with them when they had abandoned their homes and crossed the Rhine, there were also many women and children, and they then began to flee in all directions. Caesar ordered the cavalry to hunt them down.' No mercy was shown, even to those who could offer no resistance. It was not surprising that Caesar's enemies in Rome pounced on the news of this slaughter and threatened to prosecute him for war crimes. But while some in Rome may have been genuinely appalled at this action, their concern was aimed more at destroying Caesar's reputation than exacting justice for the massacre.

Throughout the wars the majority of civilian casualties probably occurred during sieges. More often than not a tribe's civilians were caught up in the assault and capture of their hill forts or *oppida*, or in the blockades that occurred more rarely. Some of these *oppida* were well defended by Celtic standards (though not by Roman), and were basically fortified towns, some of which were flourishing with substantial buildings and populations by the mid-1st century BC. Civilians naturally sought refuge within their walls when an enemy army appeared on the scene, and when their armies were defeated in the field or chose not to face the Romans in pitched battle, they too retreated to the 'safety' of their *oppida*. These fortifications rarely posed much of a challenge to the Romans, however, and the lives of those inside, whether warrior or civilian, were

Human bones showing evidence of battle trauma and swords from the Meuse at Kessel / Lith provide graphic evidence of Caesar's massacre of the Usipetes and Tencteri. (After Roymans 2018, Fig. 15.7 and 15.8. *Conflict Archaeology. Materialities of collective violence from prehistory to late antiquity*, 2018)

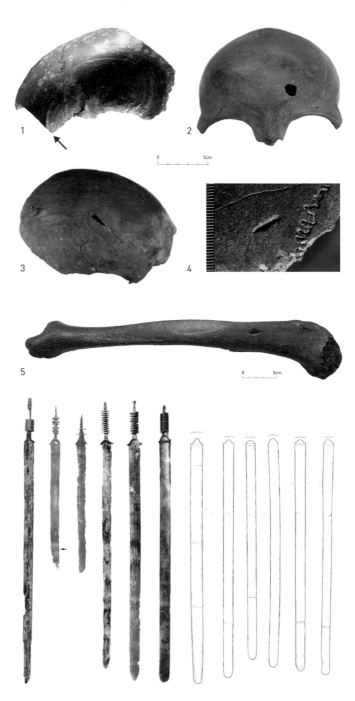

in the hands of the Roman general. Under the accepted modes of behaviour in ancient warfare, if the place surrendered, then usually the defenders and civilians caught inside were treated with leniency, but if it resisted and was taken by force or starved into surrender after a blockade, then the treatment of all might be extremely brutal. Indiscriminate slaughter followed the capture of Avaricum by assault in 52 BC with nearly 40,000 Gallic casualties, according to Caesar. Many of them were women and children. The Aduatuci escaped this fate when they surrendered their *oppidum* to Caesar in 55 BC but because they then attacked the Roman guards, Caesar had the whole population sold into slavery. Siege warfare brought a worse fate though for the civilian inhabitants of Alesia. The non-combatants of the Mandubii tribe whose town it was were thrown out of their *oppidum* by Vercingetorix, who was trying to conserve his food supplies. Caesar, following standard military procedure, refused to allow them through the Roman lines and sent them back in an attempt to hasten the Gauls' starvation and hence the end of the siege. Vercingetorix refused to allow them entry back into the town and they remained, gradually starving to death, in no-man's land within the siege works.

The Romans did not escape without losses, the most serious being the one and a half legions wiped out in the winter of 54 BC, anything from 5,000 to 7,000 men depending on how under-strength the legions were. Caesar is unusually frank about the seriousness of this defeat, mainly because he could place the blame firmly on his legate Sabinus, who had been commanding the detachment. He reports the losses at Gergovia as nearly 700, including 46 centurions, but elsewhere the general is fairly circumspect about the reverses and losses suffered by his own forces, not even providing the casualty figures from successful pitched battles which he must have known. Injuries, sickness and deaths must have reduced the strength of the legions, and by the end of the civil war with Pompey in 48 BC some of his legions were less than

two-thirds of their proper strength. But because his *Commentaries* had a propaganda purpose, Caesar deliberately downplayed most of the reverses he suffered and the casualties his forces took. Few Roman civilians were caught up in the war. Merchants and their families were massacred in Cenabum during the general uprising of 52 BC, and although there were enough of them to form an identifiable group within several towns, we can only guess at the numbers involved – probably not that many.

It is impossible to make any kind of accurate calculation of the total loss of life during the Gallic War. Gallic casualty figures are inflated for literary and political effect, whilst Roman ones are downplayed. An estimate of tens of thousands of Roman losses would probably be reasonable, while the casualty figures for the Gauls, Germans and Britons combined ran into the hundreds of thousands. Gallic warriors and men of military age are likely to have been particularly heavily hit with a resultant imbalance in the population, but the population of Gaul especially would also have been depleted by the numbers carried off into slavery.

Slavery

Slavery was a common feature of most societies in the ancient world. Rome was increasingly dependent on slavery in the late Republic with large numbers being employed in agriculture and the production of raw materials, especially in mines and quarries. Gauls also kept slaves, procuring them during raids on other tribes, and there was a thriving trade in slaves from Gaul to Rome, with luxuries and particularly wine being exchanged for them. Slaves were one of the most common acquisitions from Rome's extensive wars of conquest since prisoners of war were generally sold into slavery. An influx of Gallic slaves was probably expected when Caesar began his campaigns in 58 BC. Traditionally, the slaves taken in a campaign were the property of the commanding

OPPOSITE
The 19th-century statue of Vercingetorix by the sculptor J.G. Millet, set up at the site of Alesia by Napoleon III. (Patrick, Flickr, CC BY-SA 2.0)

Bronze figure of
Gallic prisoner
with bound hands,
Roman Imperial
period. (Photo by
CM Dixon/Print
Collector/Getty
Images)

Iron slave shackles, Hampshire, UK. Such shackles have been discovered at many rural sites in northern Europe, indicating the captive labour used in Roman agriculture. (Winchester Museum Service, CC BY 4.0)

general, and they represented one of the most lucrative immediate sources of income for him. This must have been particularly important for Caesar, who had bankrupted himself during his election campaigns for various magistracies in Rome, and especially in buying the position of *Pontifex Maximus* (Chief Priest) in 63 BC. Despite his right to possession of the slaves, Caesar was generous to his soldiers and gave them the slaves captured in some of the campaigns. This made him extremely popular with his men and increased their loyalty, an important factor in the succeeding civil war.

Caesar reports that his army captured huge numbers of prisoners during his wars of conquest and many of these were sold into slavery. He claims that 53,000 men, women and children of the Aduatuci tribe were captured when he took their *oppidum* in 57 BC, and this may have been the majority of the entire tribe.

Because of their perfidy (they had surrendered but then during the night had rallied and attacked the Romans), Caesar had all of them sold into slavery, auctioned off, and pocketed all the proceeds which must have been a vast sum. The following year he treated the Veneti in a similar manner. Many tribes who resisted Caesar escaped fairly lightly and did not have their populations taken as slaves, but the Veneti were treated differently because, like the Aduatuci, they had shown themselves to be untrustworthy in Roman eyes, detaining Caesar's envoys (admittedly sent to requisition grain supplies during the winter, which they may have felt legitimately aggrieved about given that they were not at the time subject to Rome). The Venetic elders were executed and the entire population, men, women and children (or at least those who were rounded up), were sold into slavery.

While the slaves captured during the campaigns were a useful source of much-needed wealth for Caesar, their worth lay principally in their numbers. As individual slaves they were less valuable, relatively, than slaves from other parts of the Mediterranean world, for they were unskilled. In a letter to his friend Atticus, Marcus Tullius Cicero makes a snide remark about the perceived barbarous culture of the Celts, indicating that the slaves were illiterate and 'uncivilised'. Rome had not yet reached the point when thousands of prisoners of war were sacrificed in the arena by emperors for the amusement of their subjects; many of the slaves from the Gallic wars would have been sold for their muscle, to work in the fields, in quarries and mines, often in appalling conditions with a very short life expectancy. Some, including women and children, may have ended up in Rome, but the majority were probably put to work in northern Italy, Provence and Spain.

It is just as impossible a task to estimate the numbers of Gauls enslaved as it is the casualty figures; whatever the actual numbers though, Caesar's Gallic War must have dealt a major blow to the size and balance of Gaul's population. Those not killed or captured and auctioned off as slaves by the Romans did not avoid the suffering themselves: the war brought widespread destruction and hunger.

Destruction

Ancient warfare, by its very nature, was nothing like as destructive as more modern forms of war; the demolition of property and possessions would usually have been quite well targeted, at least when sanctioned or specifically ordered by Roman officers. What we do not hear about, but must assume happened, was casual raiding, destruction and looting by Roman soldiers. They are not reported in the ancient accounts of the campaigns because of the political nature of the narrative that Caesar was producing: ill-disciplined soldiers did not reflect well on him and he wanted to tell his audience about successful operations, battles and conquest, not the minor details of soldiers looting. But we hear about such activities from narratives of other wars and campaigns from the Roman period, and there is no reason to assume that the behaviour of the Roman soldiers in Gaul was any different. As with casualties, it is impossible to quantify the amount of destruction; that carried out on orders was probably precisely directed and tribes friendly to Rome such as the Aedui and the Remi probably escaped more or less unscathed. Siege warfare obviously resulted in the destruction of a great deal of property as towns were captured and sacked, but the countryside was also devastated. The enormous siege terrace at Avaricum and extensive fortifications at Alesia must have required huge quantities of timber for their construction, and the countryside surrounding these *oppida* must have remained scarred for a generation after the conquest.

The campaigns against the Menapii and Morini were primarily destructive. Because the population withdrew into inaccessible marshes, the Romans simply destroyed all the livestock, farms and villages they could find in the hope or expectation that this would force

the Gauls into surrender. It did, for with their wealth and livelihoods gone they had no option. Despite being able to cause widespread destruction and casualties, however, Rome rarely resorted to uncontrolled ravaging of the countryside or mass slaughter as a means of defeating its enemies. In a highly emotive passage, the Roman historian Tacitus, writing in the late 1st century AD about Roman provincial policy, claims that the Romans 'made a desert and called it peace'. But in creating its empire this was not Rome's approach, as there was no point in making a province if the land was unworkable and unable to sustain a population who could pay taxes to Rome.

The Gauls, too, resorted to destruction of property: in 52 BC, the entire strategy of the revolt was based on a scorched-earth policy and the expectation that the Roman army would face such severe supply problems, especially early on in the campaigning season, that it would be forced to retreat. Given the annual problems that Caesar did face in supplying his army, this was a perfectly sound strategy, and so excess supplies of food, fields, livestock and towns with all their contents were destroyed. After the complete failure of the revolt, the following winter must have been a desperate one for the Gauls and it is likely that there was widespread famine and starvation throughout central Gaul. Many of the Gallic tribes probably suffered food shortages during the winter because of the very presence of the invading army, when military requisitioning affected both subjected and allied tribes.

Food supply

The Gallic economy was based mainly on agriculture and we have already seen how the war disrupted the lives of the population in some areas of the country through the deliberate destruction of crops and livestock. Shortages were also caused by requisitions imposed by Caesar on many of the tribes in Gaul. Although it used one of the most advanced logistical systems of any

OPPOSITE
Modern model of Caesar's siege tower at Avaricum, based on literary accounts and relief sculptures from other periods. (Photo By DEA / C. BEVILACQUA/De Agostini via Getty Images)

ancient army, the relatively slow speed of contemporary transport meant that Roman armies had to arrange the provision of additional supplies from the theatre of war or from other nearby areas. In Gaul this burden was placed partly on newly conquered tribes, but also on allies such as the Aedui, part of the price they paid for Roman support. The obligation to provide for a large standing army, unlike the Gallic armies that dispersed to their homes over the winter, put a considerable strain on the tribes. Caesar relied on the Aedui for supplies, particularly during the early campaigns before he had established clear supply routes. When trailing the migrating Helvetii in 58 BC, he was intending to divert to the Aeduan capital of Bibracte to obtain supplies from his allies, and he regularly demanded grain from defeated tribes and even allies, particularly at the start of the campaigning season when little fodder would have been available in the fields.

The heaviest demands for grain and other supplies from the Gauls came over the winter months during the closed campaigning season. The legions were put into winter quarters, usually a well-fortified encampment rather than being billeted in Gallic towns, but their stationing was carefully chosen. For the most part, legions spent the winter on the lands of newly conquered tribes to keep an eye on them, perhaps to impress on them the idea that Rome was there for good with a military presence that did not disband over the winter, and to punish the tribes for opposing Rome by forcing them to feed the occupying force over the winter. These demands could place considerable strain on a tribe's grain supply and threaten their survival. But there were no 'neutrals' in this campaign and even tribes in areas far away from the campaigning who had not even opposed the Romans might have demands made upon them. The Veneti were still an independent tribe in western Gaul who had not fought against Caesar when, during the winter of 57/56 BC, he sent officers to requisition grain. Not surprisingly they were unhappy at the demands made of them and detained the officers.

Religious and social change

Gallic tribes were already undergoing social and political change before the Roman conquest. It was caused by the interaction between the Greek and Roman culture in the south of France and the Gallic tribes of central France. The incorporation of Gaul within the Roman empire led to the emergence of a Gallo-Roman culture, a fusion of the two civilisations, but this was a gradual process of assimilation that had barely begun by the end of Caesar's campaigns. The conquest of Gaul did not lead to a fundamental shift in the balance of power in the provinces, at least at the level of the Gauls. The hierarchical structure of Gallic society suited the way Rome liked to administer its provinces, relying on existing oligarchies to rule the subject population.

This allowed provinces to be run by a Roman governor with a very small administrative staff. Pro-Roman chieftains may well have been able to maintain their positions of power and status within their tribes.

Generally, Rome did not seek to impose a particular set of religious beliefs on the peoples it conquered, and local gods were often incorporated into the Roman pantheon, usually in association with a Roman god. It was extremely rare for Rome to persecute or attempt to crush a religion it encountered in the provinces, but druidism proved to be an exception and Julius Caesar began the attempt to eradicate it. Druids had considerable influence in Gallic society that was not just confined to religion: they also had a political role and could be highly influential within their tribes. The fiercely anti-Roman Aeduan aristocrat and druid Dumnorix was able to wield considerable power, and Caesar was clearly concerned that he might attempt to seize control. The principal reason for Rome's condemnation and persecution of druidism, though, was its associations with human sacrifice:

> All the Gauls are very superstitious; so people with serious illnesses and those about to enter the dangers of battle

make or promise to burn human beings as sacrifices, and the druids officiate at these sacrifices ... When they have decided to fight a battle, they promise to dedicate the spoils that they capture in battle to Mars. If they are victorious they burn the captured animals and pile up all the other spoils at one point.

    - Caesar, *Gallic War*

A shrine at Ribemont-sur-Ancre in Picardy appears to illustrate this sacrifice of warriors defeated in battle quite clearly. The dismembered remains of over 200 people, mostly young men, were arranged around a central area, along with captured weapons, just as Caesar describes. The site was in use from the 3rd century BC but may have continued in use until the Roman conquest. The site seems to have been destroyed at that point, probably by the Romans. The poet Lucan describes how Caesar ordered the destruction of a shrine at Marseilles which displayed the skulls of sacrificial victims. Such shrines have been excavated at Roquepertuse, Glanum and Entremont in southern France. To Roman sensibilities, human sacrifice was 'barbarous' and it was inappropriate to bury the dead within the precincts of shrines, so druidism was outlawed, human sacrifice was banned and the shrines were destroyed.

Rome

As already indicated, the conquest of Gaul would have had minimal impact on the lives of most Romans whatever their status. We know that Caesar's peers, particularly his political rivals, followed his exploits, and they tried to make life difficult for him, threatening him with prosecution for war crimes and at one point attempting to have his governorship terminated. But there was also considerable excitement amongst the Roman public to hear the latest news of the campaigns, particularly the crossing to Britain: 'I look forward to receiving Britannic letters from you', Marcus Cicero wrote to a young friend, Trebatius, who was expecting to go with the expedition of 54 BC.

Caesar's rivals were right to be worried about him though. During the campaigns he received unprecedented plaudits for his successes, granted to him by the senate and people in Rome; his popularity with the ordinary people, already solid, increased. He acquired a massive fortune, having been almost bankrupt only a few years previously, and most importantly he acquired a fanatically loyal army of veteran legionaries and auxiliaries drawn from the Gauls and Germans he had been fighting against and forming alliances with. With this military strength he felt confident to risk gambling his political future and his very life, and was ready to resort to civil war to obtain the domination he felt was due to him.

HOW THE WAR ENDED

Roman triumphs

There is no single incident or date at which the Gallic War can be said to have ended. Caesar was waging war against numerous tribes who came together in 52 BC in a concerted but failed attempt to eject the Romans from their lands. Throughout the years of campaigning, the tribes had to be defeated individually or in small coalitions. Even the surrender of Vercingetorix at Alesia did not signify the end of the war, though it was the end of serious resistance to Rome, at least for the time being. Caesar portrayed Vercingetorix's surrender as the climax of his whole governorship. He had not only conquered all of Gaul, he claimed, but had completely crushed the revolt led by the charismatic Gallic chieftain, a hero worthy of his prominent position in Caesar's narrative. Caesar stopped compiling his commentaries on the war after the crushing of the revolt of 52 BC, because he had been granted a further 20 days' public thanksgiving and no longer needed to boast to those in Rome of his military successes. But the campaigns continued; Aulus Hirtius, one of Caesar's officers, continued the commentaries, taking the story down to 50 BC and the eve of civil war. Small-scale campaigns rumbled on into 50 BC and only stopped because of the needs of the civil war: Caesar took most of the garrison out of Gaul to fight against Pompey. Gaul was

not fully reduced to provincial status until the reign of the first emperor, Augustus, and even after that there are indications of the need for further campaigns. But there was no doubt who was the victor; the campaigns had been largely one-sided, and the capitulation of the tribes by the late 50s was all but total. Surrender had been unconditional.

Seven legions had marched against the Bellovaci in 51 BC, which may have been an over-reaction, but Caesar wished to make an example of those who continued to resist. He forced the surrender of Uxellodunum, an *oppidum* in south-western Gaul that was being held by the remnants of the revolt of the previous year, and punitive campaigns took place against several tribes in the north. The last military action in Gaul reported by Aulus Hirtius occurred at the end of 51 BC, after the legions had been sent to winter quarters. Commius, a chief of the Atrebates tribe who had once been an ally of Caesar but had then joined Vercingetorix, began causing problems. In the account, Aulus Hirtius claims that the Atrebates as a tribe were peaceful and submissive to Rome, and that Commius was little more than a bandit, riding around with a group of warriors disturbing the peace. The fact that Commius was actually attacking military targets, successfully ambushing supply convoys, suggests that in reality he was attempting to continue resistance, albeit on a fairly small scale. The Roman legate Volusenus was detailed to wipe out Commius and a series of encounters took place, coming to a head in a small skirmish in which Volusenus received a lance through the thigh courtesy of Commius. Commius and his followers were promptly put to flight and agreed to Roman demands that he live where told and surrender hostages to guarantee his compliance. But Aulus Hirtius does not give us the full story. A brief account by the 1st-century AD writer Frontinus claims that Commius tried to escape from the Romans in a boat but it was stranded by the low tide. The cunning Atrebatan hoisted the sails despite being grounded and

OPPOSITE
Portrait bust of Pompey, Caesar's rival in the civil wars that erupted following the conquest of Gaul. (Photo by PHAS/ Universal Images Group via Getty Images)

the pursuing Romans, believing him to be getting away, abandoned the pursuit. Commius made it to Britain where he managed to establish himself as king of the British Atrebates.

By the late 50s it had become apparent to many Gallic tribes that there was little point in further resistance to the Roman conquest, even if they had had the manpower and resources to do so. Much of the land in central Gaul had been devastated, particularly in the revolt of 52 BC when the Gauls destroyed their livestock and grain supplies in order to deny the Romans; many of the tribes who had been heavily involved in the fighting must have been short of warriors. With Roman armies wintering in Gaul and never disbanding, it was clear that, unlike most of the enemies they had faced previously, the Romans were not simply going to go away. At the time, submission must have seemed to many to be the only option short of annihilation. Viewed from two millennia away, this outcome was virtually inevitable. Caesar may have ridden his luck many times and taken some appalling risks, but the Roman army was too well trained and equipped to be defeated in such a war, too organised, with a strong command structure, logistical system (which worked well at least some of the time), and the ability to maintain an army in the field year in year out. If Caesar had not conquered Gaul, some other Roman general would have done.

The remainder of Caesar's tenure as governor was spent in conciliating the Gauls he had so recently conquered, the next stage in creating a Roman province. Civil war blocked the normal procedure: the sending out of a senatorial commission to establish the provinces, and it was not until much later that these were established by Augustus. Caesar aimed at establishing a working relationship with the tribes he had recently been fighting against, especially with the tribal elites. He bolstered the positions of those he trusted through concessions and gifts, thus ensuring their loyalty to Rome, and also to himself, something that he would benefit from in the ensuing civil war.

The tribal system was allowed to remain, based initially round the *oppida*, and these or later more Roman-style settlements nearby formed the foundations of the *civitates*, the towns of Roman Gaul on which the government and administration of the provinces were centred. A tribute was set for the subject tribes throughout Gaul that was not light, but nor was it oppressively heavy.

Public thanksgivings were offered by the Senate and People of Rome for the last time in 52 BC. Caesar had been awarded an unprecedented number of tributes for his various exploits, so his successes were being celebrated in Rome in his absence. The formal celebrations for victory in the war had to wait for years, until 46 BC, when the civil wars had run their course and Caesar had made himself dictator of Rome. Then he held a triumph; this was the procession through Rome of the successful general in a chariot, followed by tableaux illustrating the campaigns, and his troops who traditionally sang dirty songs about their commander:

> Home we bring our bald whoremonger; Romans, lock your wives away!
> All the bags of gold you lent him, went his Gallic tarts to pay.
>   - Suetonius, *Life of Caesar*, translated by Robert Graves

The Gallic triumph was one of four; the others celebrated campaigns in Turkey, Africa and Egypt. Money was given to the people of Rome who watched the procession and to the soldiers, a particularly generous amount in this instance because of their loyal support throughout the civil wars. While Caesar was the star of all four triumphs, 'second billing' in the Gallic triumph was given to Vercingetorix. The Gallic chieftain had been imprisoned in an Italian town for six years, waiting for the day of the triumph when he would be processed round the streets of Rome in chains, and then taken to the Tullianum prison in the Roman Forum to be strangled. Caesar undertook huge building

projects in Rome financed partly through his spoils from the war. He built the Temple of Venus Genetrix not only to honour the legendary divine founder of his family (and his lover Cleopatra), but also to display the spoils from his campaigns, probably weapons and particularly wealthy booty, including from Britain, to remind his fellow Romans that he had been the first to cross the 'ocean' and invade the mystical island.

Caesar's lightning campaigns and conquest of a huge area meant that some parts were not thoroughly conquered and further campaigns would be necessary. But he got out of his governorship what he had intended and what he needed to secure his political future. He had set out to make himself a fortune and a military reputation and to do that he had precipitated an encounter with the Helvetii and

The theatre in the Roman colony of Lyon founded under the emperor Augustus as a centre of Roman control and culture. (Gregory_DUBUS/ Getty Images)

The Forum Romanum in Rome with the Temple of Venus Genetrix, built by Caesar and containing spoils from his expeditions to Britain. (Peter Eastland / Alamy Stock Photo)

engineered a campaign against the Germans, giving him the excuse to conquer the whole of Gaul. He had the means by 50 BC to wage successful civil war and make himself dictator.

CONCLUSION AND CONSEQUENCES

Pax Romana

Facts and figures were an important part of any narrative of an ancient war and Caesar's account is no exception. He regularly enumerates the size and type of enemy forces he was facing and often gives a figure for their casualties. The accuracy of such figures in antiquity is notoriously unreliable simply because of difficulty in judging them and the paucity of records. In addition there were good political reasons for Caesar to exaggerate both the size of the enemy force and the number of casualties inflicted. Casualty figures were a kind of currency of military success, not least because a general needed to have inflicted at least 5,000 enemy casualties in battle in order to qualify for triumphal honours and a public procession back in Rome. So figures are likely to have been inflated to stress the military skill and prowess of the commander and his troops. The rule on minimum figures for triumphs may have encouraged the slaughter in the aftermath of battle to go on longer than strictly necessary, just to make sure enough were killed. The figures given in the *Gallic War* for sizes of enemy forces and casualties must be regarded as very rough estimates that are severely exaggerated. Sometimes they become almost unbelievable. It is highly unlikely that the Gallic relieving army at Alesia was anything like the

240,000 Caesar claims, even though to give his figures a suggestion of authenticity he lists each individual tribe and the number of warriors they contributed. Along with the alleged 80,000 Gauls trapped in the *oppidum* with Vercingetorix this represents an unlikely concentration of troops. Caesar was probably never as seriously outnumbered as he likes to suggest. Despite the problems with numbers, however, the total casualties in the nine years of fighting must have been appalling. Some tribes were all but wiped out, or else their influence declined significantly because of crushing defeats with high casualties. The Helvetii thought of themselves as one of the bravest and most influential of the Gallic tribes, but after they were forced back to their homelands little is heard of them again.

Caesar was unlikely to be criticised for killing Gauls and Germans though, especially since he managed to do it without suffering any really serious defeats himself. The one major defeat with the loss of one and a half legions in the winter of 54 BC was blamed squarely on his subordinate officer Sabinus, whom Caesar portrayed as an inept coward. As far as Caesar's fellow Romans were concerned, killing Gauls and Germans in large numbers was perfectly acceptable and usually to be praised. Both peoples had inflicted serious defeats on the Romans in the past (in the very distant past in the former case), and so the destruction of Gallic and Germanic armies by Caesar was seen simply as revenge for previous losses and a defence against anything like it ever happening again. Caesar goes to a great deal of trouble in his accounts to link the enemies of his first campaigns to tribes who had been involved in earlier defeats of Roman armies. So the Tigurini, the Helvetians massacred at the Saône in 58 BC, had defeated a Roman army in 107 BC; Ariovistus was a German king; the Aduatuci descended from the Cimbri and Teutones who had destroyed several Roman armies in the late 2nd century BC. To the Romans, these people were also barbarians, and it would not be going too far to suggest that in the Roman mentality the only good barbarian was a dead one.

The melee of pitched battle between Romans and Gauls from the decorative friezes on the early imperial triumphal arch at Orange. (Patrick, Flickr, CC BY-SA 2.0)

Despite this outlook, there were moves by some politicians in Rome to have Caesar removed from his governorship and charged with what would today be termed 'war crimes'. Charges would probably have included waging war outside his own province (which was, of course, limited to Cisalpine and Transalpine Gaul), and attacking peoples without justification, a necessary factor for a just war in antiquity. The outcry at the massacre of the Usipetes and Tencteri in 55 BC

may represent genuine repugnance at the slaughter of so many women and children on so flimsy a pretext. But it is important to remember that the men working to bring these charges against Caesar were bitter political rivals who saw him as a threat to the stability of Rome. Most of their actions to try to get Caesar removed and put on trial were motivated more by a desire to destroy him than by genuine concern for the treatment of the enemy. In his *Life of Caesar*, Suetonius noted,

He did not ignore any opportunity to wage war regardless of how unjustified it was or how dangerous. He attacked enemies and barbarians without provocation, and even allies, so eventually the Senate sent legates to report on the condition of Gaul. Several suggested that Caesar should be handed over to the enemy [for punishment for his actions].

No major advances were made by either side in military terms. The Roman style of fighting, and indeed their equipment, was entirely suitable for facing taller Celts and Germans with their long slashing blades, and the flexibility offered by the cohortal organisation of the legions was ideal for dealing with an enemy that did not maintain disciplined rank formations. Many modern historians have suggested that Caesar made alterations to the *pilum* (javelin). He is credited with fitting the *pilum* with an iron shank that was partly untempered. This ensured that it was likely to be a far less effective weapon for the enemy to throw back if the shaft had bent, and if it pierced an enemy shield and subsequently bent, it would be very difficult to extract in a hurry and might force the enemy to throw away his shield and fight unprotected. This is the effect that Caesar notes during the battle with the Helvetii and it is this observation that led modern historians to claim that he made the alterations himself. Examples of such *pila* with bent shanks have been excavated at Alesia, so clearly his reporting of the effect of the *pilum* is not only plausible but also reliable. However, there is no evidence at all to associate Caesar with any experimentation with the *pilum* or change in its design. The Roman general and consul Marius had done so previously, replacing two of the iron rivets fastening the shank to the wooden shaft with wooden pegs in order to create the same effect in a *pilum* with a fully tempered shank, but it would be wrong to credit Caesar with this further development.

Before the invasions, some Gallic hillforts or *oppida* were strengthened with larger and more extensive defences of the type Caesar describes and

experienced some difficulties with, but Rome had the siege techniques and resources to overcome them as graphically described by Caesar with the capture of Avaricum. The Gauls learned during the conquest of their lands that pitched battle was not the way to defeat the Romans: they were too well trained and disciplined to be beaten in open warfare. Hit-and-run tactics were far more effective, as were ambushes, and as the Gauls gained more experience of Roman techniques, they made more use of these methods. Crassus had encountered them first in Aquitania where the Gallic tribes were assisted by Spaniards from across the Pyrenees who had learned the effectiveness of guerrilla warfare against Roman armies when fighting for the Roman renegade Sertorius against Pompey in the 70s BC. The Gallic strategy of 52 BC was based on a scorched-earth policy, hit-and-run tactics to cut the Romans off from their supplies, and an avoidance of pitched battle. It failed because of the Romans' skill in siege warfare. Guerrilla warfare remained the most effective form of military opposition to Roman armies in western Europe, as illustrated by the spectacular success of Arminius' ambush of three Roman legions in AD 9, ending Roman hopes of the conquest of Germany.

The transition from conquered lands to provinces was a slow one. Any major advances in this direction were put on hold by the impending civil war between Caesar and Pompey, but even during his last year as governor Caesar had turned his attention back towards Rome. His actions in setting tribute were a stop-gap and although only a skeleton garrison remained in Gaul during the civil wars there is little sign of any serious attempt at an uprising: the tribes were probably still recovering from the crushing defeats inflicted by the Romans. Others, like the Aedui and Remi, must have been counting their luck that they had chosen to side with Rome. As far as possible, the existing hierarchies within tribes were maintained. Caesar did not attempt to impose a different method of rule on the Gauls but, in keeping with usual Roman policy towards provinces, preferred to work with the systems of rule that the people were used to. The Gallic tribes and their internal structures fitted in well with Rome's preference for rule by wealthy oligarchies, whether that was tribal chieftains in Gaul or elite magistrates in cities in the eastern Mediterranean. The existing tribal territories were for the most part maintained, becoming the lands administered by the towns that grew up or were established, often close to Gallic *oppida*, but generally without fortifications. 'Civilisation' had arrived.

This 'civilisation' was not forcibly imposed on the Gauls by the Romans, but during his dictatorship Caesar established a number of citizen colonies in Gaul, mostly in Provence. They served a dual purpose: providing land and retirement rewards for the soldiers who had served Caesar during the civil war, and forming a core of experienced veterans who could be called on in times of emergency, but who could also illustrate to the locals the advantages of being Roman. It was some time, however, before all the tribes in Gaul accepted this. Though Gaul seems to have remained remarkably quiet during the civil wars, it was not entirely trouble free. In 39 BC the Roman governor Agrippa (who later won the battle of Actium for Julius Caesar's great-nephew Octavian, effectively making him emperor of Rome) campaigned in the same areas of north-eastern and south-western Gaul that had never been fully settled by Caesar. Agrippa also established a road network that provided Gaul with a strong infrastructure that helped in both the continuing pacification of the area and with economic development and the spread of Roman culture. Octavian, who became the emperor Augustus, visited Gaul several times, probably increasing his prestige among the Gauls by stressing his relationship to the man who had conquered their lands. Roman camps in north-eastern Gaul may date to these campaigns, but very little is known about them. In 27 BC Augustus established three provinces probably based on the three parts of Gaul that Caesar had defined at the very beginning of his *Gallic War*. The provinces were Aquitania, Gallia Belgica and Gallia Lugdunensis, the latter having as its provincial capital the city of Lugdunum or Lyons, founded as a Roman veteran colony in 44 BC. Many of the towns that were founded as the 'capitals' of the individual Gallic tribes flourished and remain important towns in

modern France, including Soissons, Bayeux, Tours and Autun (with its Roman name Augustodunum, 'town of Augustus'), which was the new capital of the Aedui.

Further campaigns took place in the Alps between the 20s and 15 BC before Roman attention turned towards Germany. Military disaster there in AD 9 brought the frontier between Gaul in the Roman empire and Germany to more or less the line of the Rhine, and a very strong legionary force was stationed along the river. Like the new towns in Gaul, these legionary bases also left their mark on the later history of the region as most of the fortresses spawned civilian settlements that outlived the Roman empire: Strasbourg, Bonn and Mainz all began in this way. Despite the strong military presence, however, there are indications that Gaul was still not completely settled and the occasional outburst of resistance materialised. A revolt broke out in AD 21 led by two noblemen, Julius Florus, a Treveran, and an Aeduan, Julius Sacrovir, who had both commanded Roman auxiliaries and been granted Roman citizenship. The cause was very probably related to the collection of taxes, but it failed to gather widespread support and was put down with the help of other Gauls. The late 20th century discovery of a legionary fortress at Mirebeau-sur-Bèze near Dijon dating to about the AD 70s suggests that things were still not completely quiet even a century after Augustus' formal establishment of the provinces, but there is no evidence of widespread destruction. Gaul was on its way to becoming a 'Romanised' province, clearly indicated by the decision of the emperor Claudius to allow Roman citizens of Gallic ancestry to enter the senate.

Julius Caesar claimed to have conquered Gaul. He did defeat the tribes and force them to surrender, but he left Gaul still unsettled in order to pursue his personal ambitions. His fame as the conqueror of Gaul comes from his own hand, as the author of his *Commentaries*; he did not on his own turn Gaul into Roman provinces – that was for his political successors to do. The conquests

OPPOSITE
Augustodunum (Autun). Remains of a monumental early imperial temple of Janus built within and as part of a religious sanctuary dating back to Neolithic times. (Photo By DEA / G. DAGLI ORTI/De Agostini via Getty Images)

brought Gaul into the Roman empire and began a process that had a profound political and cultural impact on western Europe; and it provided Caesar with the springboard to establish himself as dictator of the Roman world.

CHRONOLOGY

390 BC	Gallic sack of Rome.
154	Marseilles, a Greek city, requests help from Rome following threats from Gallic tribes.
122	Alliance formed between Rome and the Aedui tribe. Roman campaigns against Allobroges tribe.
121	A Roman army 30,000 strong defeats a combined force of Arverni and Allobroges reportedly 200,000 strong. The Allobroges are incorporated within Roman territory. The Via Domitia road is built across southern France, linking Italy and Spain.
118	Roman colony of Narbo (Narbonne) is founded.
113–101	Invasions of Gaul and Italy by Cimbri and Teutones (Germanic tribes).
71	Rivalry between Aedui and Arverni; Arvernian allies, the Sequani, hire German mercenaries and together they defeat the Aedui.
66 & 62	Allobroges revolt, mainly because of poor Roman administration.
61	Aedui request help from Rome; Rome declines to assist but the Senate formally confirms Roman support for them. The Helvetii prepare to migrate to western France.
59	Caesar is consul (chief magistrate) in Rome; he is appointed governor of northern Italy (Cisalpine Gaul) and Dalmatia for five years. Southern France (Transalpine Gaul) is added to Caesar's jurisdiction after the sudden death of the governor.
58	Caesar takes up his governorship. March: the Helvetii begin their migration. Late June: Helvetii defeated and ordered home. Mid-September: Ariovistus defeated.
57	Campaigns against the Belgae. Winter: Roman reverse in the Alps.
56	Roman naval defeat of Veneti. Roman legate Sabinus defeats tribes of Normandy. Roman legate Crassus reduces Aquitania (south-west France). The Menapii and Morini (Belgian coast and Rhine delta) successfully resist Roman incursions. Caesar's command is extended for a further five years.

55   German tribes cross the Rhine; they are massacred by Caesar.
            The Romans bridge the Rhine. First Roman invasion of Britain.
54   Morini submit to Rome, possibly intimidated by the presence of
            the Roman fleet in the English Channel.
            Summer: second Roman invasion of Britain.
            Winter: attacks on Roman winter camps.
53   Punitive campaigns against Belgic tribes.
52   Gallic revolt.
            Winter: massacre of Roman civilians at Cenabum (Orleans).
            Spring/summer: capture of Avaricum. Gallic success at Gergovia
            and partial defection of Aedui.
            Roman successes against Parisii. Siege of Alesia; surrender of
            Vercingetorix.
51   Winter: raids on Bituriges. Roman raids against Bellovaci. Final
            defeat of Treveri. Blockade and surrender of Uxellodunum (in
            Lot, south-west France).
50   Minor Roman campaigns in central Gaul.
49   Caesar crosses the Rubicon in north Italy and civil war ensues.

FURTHER READING

Ancient sources

Translations of these works can be found easily on the internet.

Appian, *Roman History: Celtica*

Caesar, *Gallic War*

Cassius Dio, *Roman History*

Suetonius, *Life of the Divine Julius Caesar*

Plutarch, *Life of Caesar*

Modern works

Campbell, D.B., *Greek and Roman Artillery, 399 BC–AD 363*, Oxford, 2003

Campbell, D.B., *Siege Warfare in the Roman World, 146 BC–AD 378*, Oxford, 2005

Cunliffe, B., *Greeks, Romans and Barbarians*, Oxford, 1988

Drinkwater, J., *Roman Gaul*, London, 1983

Erdkamp, P., (ed.), *A Companion to the Roman Army*, Oxford, 2007

Feugere, M., *Les armes des Romains*, Paris, 1993

Fitzpatrick, A.P., & Haselgrove, C., *Julius Caesar's Battle for Gaul: New Archaeological Perspectives*, Oxford, 2019

Goldsworthy, A.K., *Caesar. The Life of a Colossus*, London, 2006

Goudineau, C., *César et la Gaule*, Paris, 1990

Griffin, M., (ed.), *A Companion to Julius Caesar*, Oxford, 2007

Holmes, T. Rice, *Caesar's Conquest of Gaul*, Oxford, 1911

Keppie, L., *The Making of the Roman Army*, London, 1984

King, A.C., *Roman Gaul and Germany*, London, 1990

Raaflaub, K., (ed,), *The Landmark Julius Caesar: The Complete Works*, New York, 2017

Raaflaub, K. & Ramsey, J.T., 'Reconstructing the Chronology of Caesar's Gallic Wars', *Histos* 11, 2017, 1–73

Reddé, M., *L'armée Romaine en Gaule*, Paris, 1996

Roth, J.P., *Roman Warfare*, Cambridge, 2009

Roymans, N., 'A Roman massacre in the far north. Caesar's annihilation of the Tencteri and Usipetes in the Dutch river area', in Fernández-Götz, M. and Roymans, N., *Conflict Archaeology. Materialities of Collective Violence from Prehistory to Late Antiquity*, London, 2017, 167–81.

Todd, M., *The Early Germans*, Oxford, 2004

INDEX